The 500 Hidden Secrets of

MUNICH

INTRODUCTION

In this book, author Judith Lohse leads you around her hometown, sharing her favourite places like she would with a good friend visiting the city. The aim of the lists she drew up is to inspire visitors as well as locals who want to discover lesser-known spots in the city, and learn all about its unique character.

In comparison to other bigger cities Munich may seem small and manageable; nevertheless life can be busy and challenging. Browsing through this guide, you'll discover the places where locals escape the hustle and bustle, from the perfect restaurant to spend a convivial evening to beautiful sites to relax in the weekend. You'll also read about the historical events that shaped the city, as well as about what's going on today. What does a typical day in the life of a Munich local look like? How is life in the city with children? And above all: what it is that makes the people of Munich love their city so much?

Much has already been written about the well-known tourist attractions in Munich, so those are not the focus of this book. The addresses and facts presented here are often lesser-known; the aim of the selection is to help you see the city and its inhabitants from a different point of view. With this guide you're ready to go on little adventures or spend some memorable evenings. There is such a thing as a unique 'Munich feeling', and that's what the author wants to convey to you.

HOW TO
USE THIS BOOK?

This guide lists 500 things you need to know about Munich in 100 different categories. Most of these are places to visit, with practical information to help you find your way. Others are bits of information that help you get to know the city and its habitants. The aim of this guide is to inspire, not to cover the city from A to Z.

The places listed in the guide are given an address, including the neighbourhood, and a number. The neighbourhood and number allow you to find the locations on the maps at the beginning of the book: first look for the map of the corresponding neighbourhood, then look for the right number. A word of caution: these maps are not detailed enough to allow you to find specific locations in the city. You can obtain an excellent map from any tourist office or in most hotels. Or the addresses can be located on a smartphone.

Please also bear in mind that cities change all the time. The chef who hits a high note one day may be uninspiring on the day you happen to visit. The hotel ecstatically reviewed in this book might suddenly go downhill under a new manager. Or the bar considered one of the '5 best places to start your pub crawl' might be empty on the night you visit. This is obviously a highly personal selection. You might not always agree with it. If you want to leave a comment, recommend a bar or reveal your favourite secret place, please visit the website *www.the500hiddensecrets.com* – you'll also find a lot of free tips and the latest news on the series there – or follow *@500hiddensecrets* on Instagram or Facebook and leave a comment.

THE AUTHOR

Judith Lohse has lived in Munich all her life. She's an avid cyclist with a curious attitude; one of her favourite pastimes is to whizz through the city's streets with her eyes wide open, looking for new and unusual places and things. Friends, neighbours and colleagues know how much she loves hearing and writing down anecdotes and little stories of Munich's everyday life. This passion resulted in her writing the city guide *München Geheim* (in German), which was awarded with the prestigious ITB Award.

In drawing up the lists of hidden secrets, the author has taken advice from friends, journalists, shopkeepers, local historians and local heroes. Many of them also accompanied her on her explorative expeditions. Judith would like to thank every one of them. She is particularly grateful to Oliver, Jakob and Samuel. Many thanks also go to Simone Schirmer for her wonderful images and to Cornelia Lettenmayer for her advice on the texts. She would like to thank the 'Secret club of Munich': Anna, Birgit, Alexandra, Nikola, Maria and Sascha, Felix, Uli, Simon and Sandra, Thomas, Martin, Mubi, Bere and Andi, Sonja and Sven, Sebastian, Sascha and Kristin, Jasmin and Anne, Marion and Oliver.

And finally, Judith would like to thank her editor Dettie Luyten and the Luster team, for their friendly support as well as their very professional approach during the entire process of making this book.

MUNICH

overview

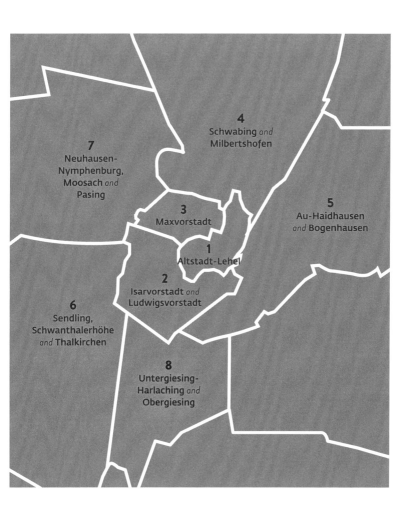

4
Schwabing *and*
Milbertshofen

7
Neuhausen-
Nymphenburg,
Moosach *and*
Pasing

5
Au-Haidhausen
and **Bogenhausen**

3
Maxvorstadt

1
Altstadt-Lehel

2
Isarvorstadt *and*
Ludwigsvorstadt

6
Sendling,
Schwanthalerhöhe
and **Thalkirchen**

8
Untergiesing-
Harlaching *and*
Obergiesing

Map 1

ALTSTADT-LEHEL

EAT — DRINK — SHOP — DISCOVER — HISTORY — CULTURE — CHILDREN — SLEEP — WEEKEND — RANDOM

Map 2
ISARVORSTADT *and*
LUDWIGSVORSTADT

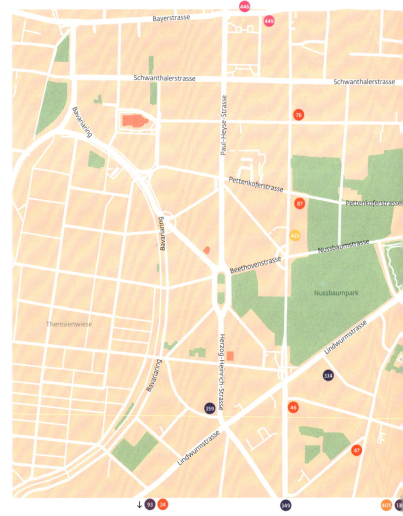

Neuhauserstrasse

Sonnenstrasse

Sonnenstrasse

Frauenstrasse

146   402

358   265

424
181

496   119
Blumenstrasse   374   191   94

143   224   335   88
45   153   426

129   216

164   248

98
216   248

377   133   138

91   365
52   454   369

414   23   16

177

360   101
126

75   205

215

125
416

227

287   49

127

30

63   29

70   13

EAT — DRINK — SHOP — DISCOVER — HISTORY — CULTURE — CHILDREN — SLEEP — WEEKEND — RANDOM

Map 3

MAXVORSTADT

EAT — DRINK — SHOP — DISCOVER — HISTORY — CULTURE — CHILDREN — SLEEP — WEEKEND — RANDOM

Map 4

SCHWABING *and* MILBERTSHOFEN

492 ↑

226

109

312

407 493

491

2R

2R

Lerchenauer Strasse

455

381

167

Luitpoldpark

403

253

Karl-Theodor-Strasse

477

309

214

Ackermannstrasse

Schleissheimer Strasse

209

20

151

77

Schwere-Reiter-Strasse

141

Schleissheimer Strasse

Elisabethstrasse

EAT — DRINK — SHOP — DISCOVER — HISTORY — CULTURE — CHILDREN — SLEEP — WEEKEND — RANDOM

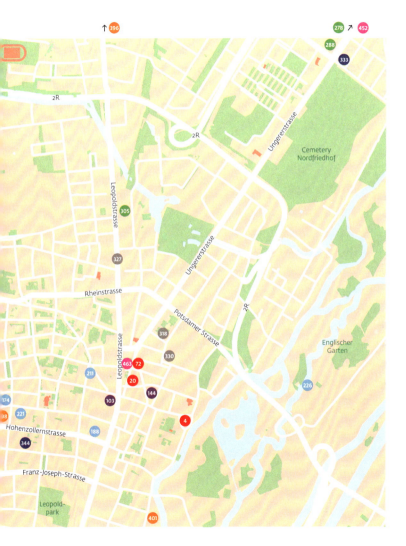

Map 5

AU-HAIDHAUSEN *and* BOGENHAUSEN

EAT — DRINK — SHOP — DISCOVER — HISTORY — CULTURE — CHILDREN — SLEEP — WEEKEND — RANDOM

Map 6

SENDLING, SCHWANTHALERHÖHE and THALKIRCHEN

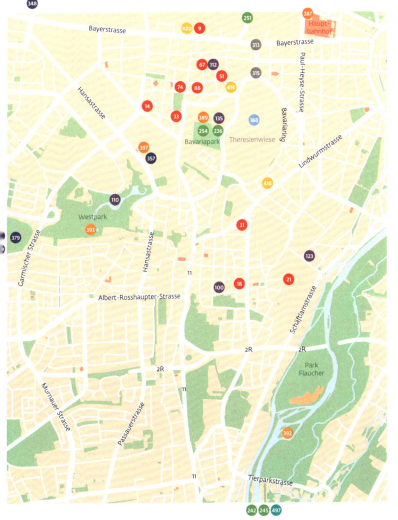

Map 7
NEUHAUSEN-NYMPHENBURG, MOOSACH and PASING

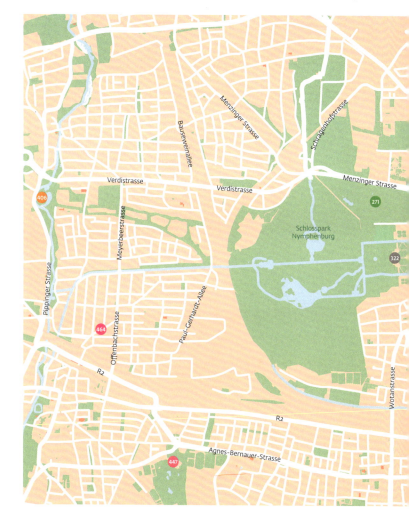

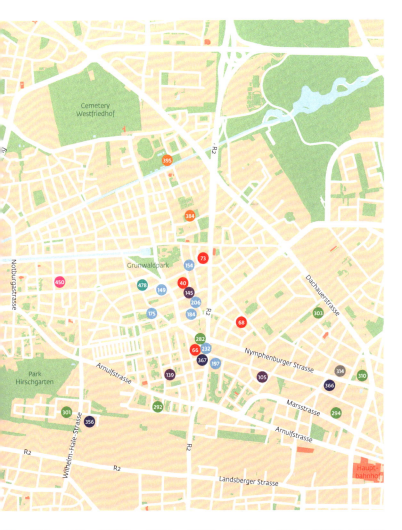

Map 8
UNTERGIESING-
HARLACHING and
OBERGIESING

Auenstrasse

Wittelsbacherstrasse

Isar

Ohlmüllerstrasse

259

Gebsattelstrasse

Falkenstrasse

Regerstrasse

212

27

Humboldtstrasse

17

274

Cemetery
Ostfriedhof

85

Tegernseer Landstrasse

116

Pilgersheimer Strasse

39

291

65

Werinherstrasse

147

Deisenhofener Strasse

404

346

2R

2R

Schönstrasse

Grünwalder Strasse

2R

385

276

EAT − DRINK − SHOP − DISCOVER − HISTORY − CULTURE − CHILDREN − SLEEP − WEEKEND − RANDOM

CONVIVA BLAUES HAUS

90 PLACES TO EAT OR BUY GOOD FOOD

5 places to have
LUNCH
like a local

1 CONVIVA BLAUES HAUS

Hildegardstrasse 1
Altstadt-Lehel ①
+49 (0)89 233 369 77
conviva-muenchen.de

The back of the restaurant is the canteen of the Münchner Kammerspiele, one of the city's leading theatres. Here actors and the theatre staff relax during the intermissions. The 'Blue House' is also a project that integrates people with special needs into the labour market. Airy atmosphere, regional cuisine.

2 KANTINE JUSTIZPALAST

Prielmayerstrasse 7
Altstadt-Lehel ①

The Bavarian Ministry of Justice is just around the corner of the city's pedestrian area. This magnificent building with its high ceilings and impressive chandeliers opens its canteen to the public every day till about 3 pm. A good place for breaks during the day.

3 KÜCHE AM ISARTOR

Lueg ins Land 1
Altstadt-Lehel ①
+49 (0)89 255 474 48
kueche-am-tor.de

This small, hidden restaurant overlooking the Isartor near the old city wall is a good place for a lunch break. The people who run it value quality ingredients. On hot days the outside terrace in the shade of the arcades is really pleasant.

4 BUSSIS KIOSK

Gunezrainer-strasse 6
Schwabing ④
+49 (0)89 242 144 44
bussis-kiosk.de

This mix of a snack bar and newsagent's is like an island between the city's hustle and bustle and the nearby Englischer Garten. The street feels like time has stood still here. As soon as the sun is out, many long-standing regulars make themselves comfortable here, including many of the eccentrics who live in Schwabing

5 VALENTIN KARLSTADT MUSÄUM

Im Tal 50
Altstadt-Lehel ①
+49 (0)89 293 762
valentin-musaeum.de

The Valentin Karlstadt Museum is dedicated to two Munich comedians Karl Valentin and Liesl Karlstadt and their peculiar style of humour. Located in the historic city gate of Isartor, you'll find a tiny cafe in the turret that serves homemade cakes and typically Bavarian snacks. A real gem!

5 VALENTIN KARLSTADT MUSÄUM

5 very
STYLISH
restaurants

---

6 NENI

Bahnhofplatz 1
Altstadt-Lehel ①
+49 (0)89 904 001 561
nenimuenchen.de

Neni München is part of the 25hours Hotel The Royal Bavarian, across the road from the main station. Their fusion of Israeli, Romanian and Spanish cuisine, the high ceilings and the rather dark, stylish ambience are very popular with the locals. Enjoy the *Balagan* style of sharing your meals.

7 PAGEOU

Kardinal-Faulhaber-
Strasse 10
Altstadt-Lehel ①
+49 (0)89 242 313 10
pageou.de

This small design restaurant at the back of the Fünf Höfe has a clear, bright interior and a nice green courtyard. Here you can enjoy fine cuisine by Michelin-Star chef Ali Güngörmüş, served by very friendly and competent staff.

8 THE SPICE BAZAAR

Marstallplatz 3
Altstadt-Lehel ①
+49 (0)89 255 477 77
thespicebazaar.de

Seen from the street, The Spice Bazaar seems a little forbidding at first, but once you step inside, the nice interior design makes you feel immediately comfortable. The cuisine here is Mediterranean-oriental – with a menu with three sections, i.e., 'briefly grilled', 'slowly cooked' and 'rawly marinated'. All meat as well as most of the other ingredients are organic.

9 **IZAKAYA**

Landsberger Str. 68
Schwanthaler-
höhe ⑥
+49 (0)89 122 232 000
izakaya-restaurant.
com

This restaurant has an open kitchen where you can watch the chefs at work, as they create their Japanese-South American fusion dishes. Just order a bit of everything – sushi, fish, seafood and meat as well as vegetarian alternatives – and share. Beware though of the giant wooden fish mobile above your head!

10 **BRENNER**

Maximilianstrasse 15
Altstadt-Lehel ①
+49 (0)89 452 2880
brennergrill.de

At the centre of this large open restaurant with its many columns you'll find the show-cooking grill station. The atmosphere is a cross between that of a grand-ducal palazzo and an old coffee house. This is where Munich's in-crowd meets, and they know why.

6 NENI

5 ×

ITALY IN MUNICH

---

11 PIZZESCO

**Rosenheimer-
strasse 12
Au-Haidhausen ⑤
+49 (0)89 679 728 12
www.pizzesco.com**

This bar looks inconspicuous but serves one of the best pizzas in town. You can have pizza slices to go or make yourself comfortable at one of the few available tables. The choice includes Kamut pizza, gluten or lactose free pizza to pizza made from spelt flour, topped with some real Italian flair.

12 CAFE MORSO

**Nordendstrasse 17
Maxvorstadt ③
+49 (0)171 307 5466
morso-cafe.de**

It's as simple as that. For many Munich residents, a real Italian bar has become a part of their daily lives. They often say: "Munich is the northernmost city of Italy". In a bar like Cafe Morso, you can enjoy excellent coffee, practise your language skills for your next vacation and feel like an Italian.

13 IL PICCOLO PRINCIPE

**Kapuziner-
strasse 48
Isarvorstadt ②
+49 (0)89 721 3450**

A bistro with bar tables and a back room with tables to sit at. At Il Piccolo Principe you'll feel as if you've just sat down in the kitchen of an Italian *mamma*. The food is fresh, made with classic ingredients. Definitely try the tiramisu for dessert. The classics taste particularly good here.

14 TRATTORIA AL PALADINO

Heimeranplatz 1
Schwanthaler-
höhe ⑥
+49 (0)89 502 5657
alpaladino.de

Lots of chandeliers and magnificent decoration. This place loves to keep it festive and celebrates Italy's finest export: good food. They pay special attention to the preparation of their appetizers. A cosy place for a great evening, as a couple or in a small group.

15 RESTAURANT LA FATTORIA

Schlotthauer-
strasse 16
Au-Haidhausen ⑤
+49 (0)89 622 314 96

You won't find pizza here. Instead they serve a small selection of fish and meat dishes as well as pasta, all equally delicious. If you'd like to have a glass of wine, just trust the owner's recommendations. There is no wine list. This restaurant has a rather minimalist interior but many guests have been coming back here for years.

11 PIZZESCO

5 places for
LOCAL FAST FOOD

16 **BERGWOLF**
Fraunhoferstrasse 17
Isarvorstadt ②
+49 (0)89 232 598 58

Not strictly Bavarian but typically German fast food. Bergwolf serves *Currywursts* to the night owls in Glockenbachviertel. The grilled pork sausage is cut into slices and served with a sauce made of ketchup and curry powder. With a serving of fries and the last beer for the night. On weekends, they are open until 4 am.

17 **TÜRKITCH**
Humboldtstrasse 20
Untergiesing-
Harlaching ⑧
+49 (0)89 890 569 63

You'll find doner kebab all over town but the fans of this Turkish snack stand are so enthusiastic about this snack they will travel for miles to get here. Whether you try a *kofta* sandwich, a turkey-vegetable kebab, a *falafel durum* or *sukuk* burger, the taste is simply delicious, and all the ingredients are homemade.

18 **BEIRUTBEIRUT**
Valleystrasse 28
Sendling ⑥
+49 (0)89 520 369 16
beirutbeirut.de

A genuine slice of Lebanon in the centre of Munich, this tiny, authentic restaurant serves homemade falafel and other Lebanese specialities. Set in a pleasantly calm neighbourhood it is soothingly different. On a sunny day, just grab a sandwich and head to the nearby park.

19 **SABABA**
Westenrieder-
strasse 9
Altstadt-Lehel ①
+49 (0)89 232 378 81
sababa-munich.com

This snack bar is tucked away at the far end of Viktualienmarkt. They serve a wide array of different oriental specialities such as *shawarma* (spicy turkey), *kebeh* (bulgur dumplings with minced meat), *labneh* (yoghurt-like cheese) or *falafel*. The food is served either on plates or as a sandwich. Don't be put off by the line of people. They have a huge fan base.

20 **CONDESA**
Münchner Freiheit 6
Schwabing ④
+49 (0)176 202 271 36
condesa-gourmet-
tacos.de

Condesa serves authentic Mexican street food that gives you that special holiday feeling with *burritos*, *quesadillas* and *tacos* of outstanding quality, that are all freshly made. The homemade guacamole is a real experience.

18 BEIRUTBEIRUT

5 authentic
BAVARIAN
restaurants

---

21 GASTSTÄTTE GROSSMARKTHALLE

**Kochelseestrasse 13
Sendling ⑥
+49 (0)89 764 531
gaststätte-
grossmarkthalle.de**

This *Gaststätte* opens at seven in the morning and closes early in the afternoon, because it mainly serves the workers of the nearby wholesalers' market. Everything here is down to earth in a traditional way. Meat products are provided by the in-house butcher. His *Weisswurst* (veal sausage) is among the best in the city.

22 KLINGLWIRT

**Balanstrasse 16
Au-Haidhausen ⑤
+49 (0)89 856 761 99
klinglwirt.de**

Gemütlichkeit is what comes to mind the moment you step into this charming place. Guests will enjoy the cordial atmosphere and the high-quality traditional food. The kitchen uses regional ingredients wherever possible and organic meat only.

23 FRAUNHOFER

Fraunhoferstrasse 9
Isarvorstadt ②
+49 (0)89 266 460
fraunhofertheater.de

Nothing much has changed here over the past centuries. This is what the Fraunhofer has always looked like and why it is truly loved by the locals. It has a classic interior, decorative ceilings and long tables to be shared with strangers. It can get rather crowded in the evenings.

24 GOLDMARIE

Schmellerstrasse 23
Isarvorstadt ②
+49 (0)89 516 692 72
goldmarie-
muenchen.de

When Bavarian cuisine meets Austrian cuisine, there is something for everyone's taste. Including roast pork or South Tyrolean *Kasnocken*. Goldmarie is the home of Alpine cooking. Sit down and enjoy a pleasant meal in their unpretentious dining area with beautiful wooden furniture.

25 BEIM SEDLMAYR

Westenrieder-
strasse 14
Altstadt-Lehel ①
+49 (0)89 226 219
beim-sedlmayr.de

Sedlmayr stands for traditional Bavarian cuisine at its best. They combine high-quality ingredients with a slow preparation. Here you'll be able to order Bavarian dishes that have become rare on menus. And the ambience makes both local and visitors' hearts beat faster.

5 great places to
SWING THROUGH SUNDAY

---

26 DIE WALDMEISTER MÜNCHEN

Barer Strasse 74
Maxvorstadt ③
+49 (0)89 189 469 56

The interior of Die Waldmeister München with its soft, muted colours, old wooden furniture and many other beautiful details is a great place to take a break and relax. In addition to a nice breakfast selection you can also get a tasty lunch here. They also do takeaway.

27 MISS LILLY'S

Oefelestrasse 12
Untergiesing-Harlaching ⑧
+49 (0)89 550 621 95
misslillys.de

Nice and bright, with a fireplace in the corner to warm you up on cold days. They serve breakfast until 5 pm and have fantastic homemade cakes. The menu changes daily. There's always something for everyone to munch through the leisurely day.

28 CAFE LUITPOLD

Brienner Strasse 11
Altstadt-Lehel ①
+49 (0)89 242 8750
cafe-luitpold.de

A coffee house with a long tradition, Cafe Luitpold is now also an exclusive restaurant. They serve the finest cakes and chocolates here. Do try the 'Luitpold cake', a speciality of this chic eatery. A small museum on the first floor tells you more about the cafe's history.

29 **DAS MARIA**
Klenzestrasse 97
Isarvorstadt ②
+49 (0)89 202 457 50
dasmaria.de

Breakfast at Das Maria is like taking a little trip around the world. They serve both oriental and American-inspired food here. The same goes for the lunch and dinner menu. The cafe is very popular in the area. No space for a pram.

30 **CAFÉ HÜLLER**
Eduard-Schmid-Strasse 8
Isarvorstadt ②
+49 (0)89 189 387 13
cafe-hueller.jimdo.com

Connoisseurs come to Café Hüller because of the excellent German-style pancakes. Whether sweet or savoury, the filling pancakes are always delicious here. There are plenty of other good homecooked options as well, of course. A welcoming, quiet place.

30 CAFÉ HÜLLER

5 homey places for
BREAKFAST

---

31 CAFÉ ERIKA
Senserstrasse 7
Sendling ⑥
+49 (0)89 452 371 38
cafe-erika.de

Lots of wooden furniture makes the interior of Café Erika very enjoyable. In addition to various classics to everyone's taste, they also serve specialities such as porridge or smoothie bowls. In summer, the garden is transformed into a small terrace.

32 KAFFEEKÜCHE
Weissenburger Strasse 6
Au-Haidhausen ⑤
+49 (0)89 461 398 47
kaffeekueche.net

For this small oasis of well-being you gladly take the extra walk. The staff are good-tempered, the food tastes lovely, they serve great coffee and various other drinks, of course. Regional meets delicious! Get here early and watch the city wake up.

33 CAFE LOHNER UND GROBITSCH
Sandtnerstrasse 5
Schwanthaler-höhe ⑥
+49 (0)89 693 092 50
lohnerundgrobitsch.de

Once a grocery store, this bright cafe serves good home-cooking. Unpretentious and a great place to start the day for all who find their way here.

34 **FRITZI MASSARY**
Dachauer Str. 54
Maxvorstadt ③
+49 (0)89 452 052 64
fritzi-massary.com

Named after an opera singer of the thirties, this cafe with its living room atmosphere has a small breakfast menu. They are well known for their special sandwiches. Good to know for early birds: they open at 8 o'clock in the morning.

35 **GARTENSALON**
Türkenstrasse 90/
Amalienpassage
Maxvorstadt ③
+49 (0)89 287 786 04
gartensalon.net

This cafe is not visible from the street, you enter through the arcades. Here you'll be rewarded with a vegetarian breakfast in a very beautiful courtyard. In addition to the many delicious treats, they sell homemade food and unusual sweets to take away.

34 FRITZI MASSARY

The 5 best
BAKERIES

36 **OBORI**
Lothringer Str. 15
Au-Haidhausen ⑤
+49 (0)89 441 426 66

This bakery produces cakes, pastries and bread of the finest quality. The shop is often sold out, that's how popular it is in the area. The Japanese owners came to Germany twenty years ago to learn the baker's trade and made their home here.

37 **KARNOLL'S BACKSTANDL**
Viktualienmarkt 6
Altstadt-Lehel ①
+49 (0)89 260 7931
karnoll-standl.de

Pretzels are an important part of Bavarian meals. Hence the many discussions about which of the city's bakeries produces the best one. Karnoll's Backstandl, in Viktualienmarkt, tops the list for many locals.

38 **BROTMANUFAKTUR SCHMIDT**
Steinstrasse 27
Au-Haidhausen ⑤
+49 (0)89 459 912 23

This bakery has been run by the same family for just under 150 years. In addition to traditional bakery goods, you'll also find delicious snacks here. Give *Krapfen* a try – Bavaria's answer to doughnuts, a pastry that is not just eaten at carnival.

39 HARALD'S BROTLADEN
Winterstrasse 15
Untergiesing ⑧
+49 (0)89 651 6090

This small shop sells pastry, some of which is produced on the premises. Have a pretzel or try one of the cakes. The range changes all the time and is worth a try on any day.

40 NEULINGER
Volkartstrasse 48
Neuhausen-Nymphenburg ⑦
+49 (0)89 188 714

If you are looking for a traditional bakery, this is the place to be. Everything is just the way the people of Munich love it: the smells, the tastes, the set-up of the shop... Heaven on earth for bread, rolls and cakes, full stop!

36 OBORI

5 spots for
VEGETARIAN & VEGAN
cooking

---

41 **IGNAZ**
Georgenstrasse 67
Maxvorstadt ③
+49 (0)89 271 609 3
ignaz-cafe.de

This cafe has been serving vegetarian and vegan food for decades. Overall, the menu is rather traditional. The weekend brunch with a wide selection of sweet and savoury foods is very popular.

42 **MAX PETT**
Pettenkoferstr. 8
Altstadt-Lehel ①
+49 (0)89 558 691 19
max-pett.de

This vegan restaurant is somewhat hidden and yet centrally located. The food is a colourful mix of regional and Asian influences. They don't serve alcohol here, which is quite unusual for a Munich restaurant.

43 **PRINZ MYSHKIN**
Hackenstrasse 2
Altstadt-Lehel ①
+49 (0)89 265 596
prinzmyshkin.com

You'll enjoy the fine vegetarian and vegan cuisine in this restaurant. The high vaulted ceiling radiates elegance. They go to great lengths to satisfy even the most fastidious vegetarian. The menu includes both on Italian and Indian dishes.

44 KISMET

Löwengrube 10
Altstadt-Lehel ①
+49 (0)89 220 352
kismet.cc

This restaurant serves a younger, somewhat hip crowd and offers a variety of oriental-inspired dishes such as *mezze* or *tajine*. A staircase leads to the first floor, where you can sit at the bar for an after-dinner drink. The upstairs area with its glass roof resembles a greenhouse.

45 JACK GLOCKENBACH

Thalkirchner
Strasse 3
Isarvorstadt ②
+49 (0)89 121 251 52
jack-glockenbach.de

Strictly speaking not a purely vegetarian restaurant. Jack Glockenbach is labeled 'vegetarian friendly' because of its varied menu. The food is tasty and looks terrific, the ambience very laidback. A good starting point to explore the city.

5 exceptional
A S I A N
restaurants

---

46 TENGRI TAGH UYGHUR RESTAURANT
Häberlstrasse 1
Isarvorstadt ②
+49 (0)89 552 716 43

Munich has the largest Uyghur community outside of China. Their traditional cuisine has Chinese, oriental and Turkish influences. *Lagman* is the name of the thick hand-drawn noodles in the various dishes on the menu. The ambience is more snack bar than restaurant.

47 J-BAR
Maistrasse 28
Isarvorstadt ②
+49 (0)89 514 699 83

The J-Bar is set up like an *izakaya*, a type of Japanese pub. Here they serve traditional specialities (so please do not ask for sushi), such as Kirin beer with iced foam. The place has a really special atmosphere and is equally popular with the Japanese and with locals. Attention: cash only.

48 SANSARO SUSHI
Amalienstrasse 89
Maxvorstadt ③
+49 (0)89 288 084 42
sushiya.de

At Sansaro Sushi, they adhere to high standards and strongly believe in a good eating experience. Real Japanese chefs working with high-quality ingredients (organic where possible) serve sushi and sashimi, but you can also order a selection of warm dishes. A special place, a special treat.

49 KIRSCHBLÜTE

Ickstattstrasse 26
Isarvorstadt ②
+49 (0)89 202 076 50

If you want to spend a nice evening in a relaxed atmosphere, then this is the place for you: Kirschblüte (cherry blossom) serves two Vietnamese mains every day, as well as some starters and desserts. Everything here has a special charm.

50 GYOZA BAR

Augustenstrasse 47
Maxvorstadt ③
+49 (0)89 203 466 47
gyozabar.de

The simple menu – they serve Chinese *gyoza* with different fillings or *wantan* in soup, the friendly service and an international crowd make for a pleasurable experience. Ideally suited for a quick bite to eat before your evening continues elsewhere. They are open every day.

47   J-BAR

5 delights for
CAKE LOVERS

51 **DAS NEUE KUBITSCHECK**
Gollierstrasse 14
Schwanthaler-
höhe ⑥
+49 (0)89 726 692 22
cafe-kubitscheck.de

No ready-mixed cakes here! The owner is a firm believer in the 'culture of cake'. This contemporary and cosy place will make you instantly happy on a dreary morning. Everything is made fresh and from scratch. Their cakes look absolutely stunning.

52 **TABULA RASA**
Holzstrasse 18
Isarvorstadt ②
+49 (0)151 252 589 24
cafetabularasa.de

You might come here for breakfast or for the fabulous lasagne but be sure not to miss the homemade cakes! Tabula Rasa is located in the heart of the trendy Glockenbachviertel. Inside, the cafe is rather small, but cosy. In summer, you might sit on the terrace in the shade, well, on the pavement under a big tree, but it's a really lovely place.

53 CAFFÈ SIENA INSIDE F.S. KUSTERMANN

Viktualienmarkt 8
Altstadt-Lehel ①
+49 (0)89 237 250

This cafe is tucked away in a long-established homewares shop. It's rather tiny so you may have to do the rounds of the shop again before you'll get a chance to sit down. But it's so worth it! The cakes taste delicious and are served on porcelain by old-fashioned waiters.

54 KONDITOREI KAFFEE SCHNELLER

Amalienstrasse 59
Maxvorstadt ③
+49 (0)89 281 124

An old-fashioned little cafe, that is popular both with students of the nearby university and long-time residents of Maxvorstadt alike. On the right-hand side of the bar, a small staircase leads to a back room where you can sit comfortably. It's all about cake, not the decor. Everything is homemade.

55 CAFÉ ARZMILLER

Salvatorstrasse 2
Altstadt-Lehel ①
+49 (0)89 294 273
cafe-arzmiller.de

The peculiar and the traditional go hand in hand in this place. Older gentlemen, who have been meeting here for decades, sit next to young families. The cafe exudes a slightly upscale atmosphere. Try *Esterhazy chocolate Gugelhupf* or *plum bavese* for a piece of heaven.

The 5 best places to
EAT AT THE MARKET

56 FISCH HÄUSL
Wiener Platz 9
Au-Haidhausen ⑤

The little market in Wiener Platz is special because elitist Munich is somehow far away. Here you can enjoy the legendary Bavarian cheerfulness. Most of the people who shop here are locals. The little market is also home to the Fisch Häusl, where they sell fresh fish as well as excellent snacks.

57 SCHLAGBAUER
Viktualienmarkt
Altstadt-Lehel ②
+49 (0)89 516 172 90
georg-schlagbauer.de

Eight butchers have been selling their specialities side by side for over 700 years now on Viktualienmarkt's 'row of butchers'. Go to Schlagbauer for a slice of *Leberkäse* in a roll. This is one of the most traditional snacks we have. The butcher sells meat from animal-friendly free-range farms only.

58 SUPPENKÜCHE

**Viktualienmarkt
Altstadt-Lehel ①
+49 (0)89 260 95 99
muenchner-
suppenkueche.de**

On cold and wet days especially, a soup will make you feel nice and warm inside. Find your way through the maze of stalls in Viktualienmarkt and try the soups, stews, curries and more. The menu lists more than a dozen homemade soups, including classics like coconut-carrot-ginger soup.

59 CASA SARDA

**Elisabethmarkt,
Stand 13
Schwabing ③
+49 (0)89 273 715 98**

Do not miss the market in Elisabethplatz. A gem in the middle of Schwabing, where time seems to have stopped. In addition to some nice delicatessen, you'll find seats in the shade and a nice playground. Casa Sarda oozes Italian flair and serves yummy Sardinian-Italian home-cooking.

60 KLEINER OCHS'NBRATER

**Viktualienmarkt 11
Altstadt-Lehel ①
+49 (0)89 298 282
kleinerochsnbrater.de**

Come here for an organic beef sandwich, it's as regional as it gets. The animals are raised on an estate on the other side of the city, which is owned by the city council. They serve unfiltered organic beer on tap in little beer garden right in the middle of Viktualienmarkt.

5 locations for
ORGANIC FOOD *and*
REGIONAL COOKING

61 SIR TOBI

Sternstrasse 16
Altstadt-Lehel ①
+49 (0)89 324 948 25
sirtobi-muenchen.de

You might not expect a cosy restaurant like this here. They serve alpine specialities such as schnitzel or *Käsespätzle*. Come here for their down-to-earth, delicious cooking that is slow food-certified. Very popular in the neighbourhood.

62 SEIDELEI

Reitmorstrasse 3
Altstadt-Lehel ①
+49 (0)89 255 422 20
seidelei.com

A place where you can enjoy a seasonal menu of fine alpine cuisine and assorted wines. All set in a relaxed atmosphere. The interior is rustic, yet contemporary. The owner will tell you about the food and help you choose a wine. Prepare to enjoy a really nice evening.

63 RUMPLER

Baumstrasse 21
Isarvorstadt ②
+49 (0)89 200 352 78
rumpler-augustiner.de

This is a very straightforward place, with a no-frills interior, dimmed light and plain wooden tables. Local ingredients and organic meat on the menu. You'll always feel at ease here, also with children. On warm days, you can sit outside and enjoy a relaxed evening in the neighbourhood. Cash only.

64 HERRMANNS-DORFER AM VIKTUALIENMARKT

Frauenstrasse 6
Altstadt-Lehel ①
+49 (0)89 263 525
herrmannsdorfer.de

The company was the first to supply high-quality organic meat and now operates several shops in Munich, as well as two bistros, one of them here in the city centre. Sit at bar tables while you watch the chef prepare your meal. Definitely worth the wait, this is a good place for a tasty lunch break.

65 DER DANTLER

Werinherstrasse 15
Obergiesing ⑧
+49 (0)89 392 926 89
derdantler.de

They call themselves a Bavarian deli and serve food that combines various alpine influences, with a creative twist. They only use sustainable ingredients, some are even produced on the premises. Try their Bavarian interpretation of *ramen* soup. Closed on weekends and Friday evenings.

65   DER DANTLER

5 restaurants for
EXCEPTIONAL COOKING

66 **BROEDING**
Schulstrasse 9
Neuhausen-
Nymphenburg ⑦
+49 (0)89 164 238
broeding.de

Their mission is to serve 'clarity and precision in the restaurant, on the plate and in the glass'. They offer one daily changing menu with five or six courses. They have received praise from the New York Times for their fantastic food and excellent wines.

67 **L'ADRESSE 37**
Tulbeckstrasse 9
Schwanthaler-
höhe ⑥
+49 (0)89 622 321 19
ladresse37.de

This warm yet elegant place serves French cuisine with a twist. Where possible, they work with sous-vide cooking. The interior is convivial and slightly sophisticated, with a view of the open kitchen. In summer they open the lovely, small courtyard for guests.

68 **ZAUBERBERG**
Hedwigstrasse 14
Neuhausen-
Nymphenburg ⑦
+49 (0)89 189 991 78
restaurant-
zauberberg.de

This gourmet restaurant serves elegant yet down-to-earth European cuisine. The perfect place for a relaxed evening, where you can unwind while enjoying the individual courses and accompanying wines. In summer, the green terrace is a very romantic spot.

69 LES DEUX

Maffeistrasse 3-A
Altstadt-Lehel ①
+49 (0)89 710 407 373
lesdeux-muc.de

This eating house has two areas: the brasserie on the ground floor and the restaurant on the first floor. In the brasserie you'll find everything from breakfast to dinner, throughout the day. The upstairs restaurant has been awarded a Michelin star and serves exquisite cuisine. The building is worth seeing in any case and dining here is always a pleasure.

70 SHANE'S RESTAURANT

Geyerstrasse 52
Isarvorstadt ②
+49 (0)89 746 468 20
shanesrestaurant.de

Shane McMahon serves European-Asian fusion cuisine in his spacious restaurant, which is located in a hotel. There is no menu. The staff will simply ask you what food you don't like and whether or not you are allergic to anything. You'll be served a creative and down-to-earth menu.

5 spots that have
ALWAYS BEEN HERE

---

71 **ZUM KLOSTER**
Preysingstrasse 77
Au-Haidhausen ⑤
+49 (0)89 447 056 4

This tavern is situated in an enchanted corner of Haidhausen. The picturesque tiny houses around the restaurant tell of old times when day labourers and craftsmen tried to survive in Munich. Inside they have two pleasant sitting areas. Outside, on a sunny spring day, a light shower of cherry blossoms might float down on you while you watch the world go by.

72 **CAFÉ MÜNCHNER FREIHEIT**
Münchner
Freiheit 20
Schwabing ④
+49 (0)89 330 079 90
muenchner-freiheit.de

Generations of young people from Munich have had their first date here. And they still come here. At the table next to them the old folks (who once met here) sit and eat their cake. Grab a chair and enjoy a slice of everyday Munich life.

73 **RUFFINI**
Orffstrasse 22-24
Neuhausen-
Nymphenburg ⑦
+49 (0)89 161 160
ruffini.de

The restaurant is run by 25 shareholders – one of them may even serve you your cup of coffee. Where possible, decisions are taken by consensus, and this has been the case ever since the seventies. Ruffini is a tribute to Italian cuisine. No using your cell phone. Timeless.

74 CAFÉ CA VA

**Kazmairstrasse 44
Schwanthaler-
höhe ⑥
+49 (0)89 502 8584
cafe-cava.de**

This pub has always been popular with younger people in the Westend. The living-room atmosphere, the dark, wooden furniture and the hearty cuisine make this a place where you can forget about time (and your own age) while ordering another beer with your garlic baguette.

75 GASTSTÄTTE FAUN

**Hans-Sachs-Str. 17
Isarvorstadt ②
+49 (0)89 263 798
faun.mycosmos.biz**

Don't be fooled by the art nouveau ambience. This isn't a place for pretentious people, but a restaurant for everyone. When crowded, it can get rather loud inside, so try to grab an outdoor table in the summertime. Just sit down, enjoy a *Helles Bier* and some people watching. When hungry, try the *Schweinebraten* and *Kaiserschmarrn*.

74 CAFÉ CA VA

5 places for
EXOTIC
food

---

76 SARA RESTAURANT
Landwehrstrasse 42
Ludwigsvorstadt ②
+49 (0)89 242 699 37

Come here if you enjoy Lebanese cuisine and would like to spend a short culinary holiday. They have their own in-house bakery, making their own flatbread (*nan*), which is served with dishes like flash-fried chicken, lamb or kebab skewers. A straightforward place, for a relaxed meal.

77 MATAJI'S KITCHEN
Schleissheimer
Strasse 121
Schwabing ④
+49 (0)89 660 796 55
matajis-kitchen.de

Yes, you can find good Indian cuisine in Munich. Be warned however that sometimes it may take a while before your meal is served. But if you come with time on your hands, you can spend a lovely and tasty evening here.

78 BLUE NILE
Viktor-Scheffel-
Strasse 22
Schwabing ④
+49 (0)89 330 399 87

Be ready to eat with your hands in this Ethiopian restaurant, where you eat the meat and vegetable dishes with pieces of sourdough pancake instead of cutlery. Although strange at first, it will soon feel very natural. Delicious food served in a relaxed atmosphere.

79 NANA

Metzstrasse 15
Haidhausen
+49 (0)89 444 996 33
nana-muenchen.de

Come here for meze, hummus or *shakshouka*. Have an accompanying Maccabi lager and enjoy your culinary trip to Israel. This friendly place, with its colourful interior, is a good spot for a lovely and tasty lunch or dinner. The owners are really nice. They also serve some extraordinary drinks.

80 NASCA

Enhuberstrasse 1
Maxvorstadt ③
+49 (0)89 523 105 94
nasca-cafe.de

Peruvian food in a bar-like atmosphere. Start your evening with a *pisco sour* and check out the unusual dishes on the menu, such as the typically Peruvian *ceviche* or raw fish marinated in lemon juice and spices. Or you could try the *quinoa paella* and many other delicacies.

The 5 best
ICE-CREAM
parlours

---

81 **EISDIELE TRAMPOLIN**
Nordendstrasse 62
Schwabing ④
+49 (0)176 785 992 10
trampolin-eis.com

Here they only use the best ingredients, no substitutes at all and they swear by organic milk only. The fruit ice-cream varieties are especially tasty.

82 **ADRIA**
Türkenstrasse 59
Maxvorstadt ③

Italian ice-cream parlours have dominated the ice-cream landscape in Munich for decades. This one is particularly charming. Get your cone and cross the street. Here you can enjoy your *gelato* in the shade of chestnut trees.

83 **BAYERISCHE EISMANUFAKTUR**
Oettingenstrasse 42-A
Altstadt-Lehel ①
+49 (0)89 255 470 34
bayerische-eismanufaktur.de

This ice-cream parlour near the English Garden uses only the best-quality, local ingredients and serves a wide variety of flavours like salty caramel ice cream. If you want something other than ice cream, then order a *granita* or a cappuccino.

84 **EIS WILHELM**
Lenbachplatz 7
Altstadt-Lehel ①

This place is run by the nearby Herzog restaurant, which is why their creations are inspired by drinks. Every ice cream comes with a topping. The house speciality is cake burger filled with ice cream.

85 **ARTEFREDDA**
Tegernseer
Landstrasse 38
Obergiesing ⑧
+49 (0)89 649 627 05
artefredda.de

Small but nice, this ice-cream parlour has divided the counter into two sections. On the left, you'll find the regular ice creams, on the right, their organic varieties featuring special ingredients, some of which are sweetened with stevia instead of sugar. A fun place for everyone with a sweet tooth.

5 hearsay
FAVOURITES

86 WEINWIRTSHAUS ZUM SCHÖNFÄRBER

Kazmairstrasse 28
Schwanthaler-
höhe ⑥
+49 (0)89 209 305 69
zum-schoenfaerber.de

They call the owner a wine saint. Here it's all about the wine (rather than the beer), but the attitude is still very down to earth. A place where they serve simple but good food and where guests are treated like friends. There is a bar area (painted red) and a restaurant area (painted green).

87 CONTECANTINA

Goethestrasse 41
Ludwigsvorstadt ②
+49 (0)89 120 245 08

ConteCantina is a nice little cafe that serves homebaked cakes and treats, *pide* and sandwiches. At lunch they have a variety of dishes on the menu. A nice place near the buzzing Hauptbahnhof area.

88 KÖNIGSQUELLE

Baaderplatz 2
Isarvorstadt ②
+49 (0)89 220 071
koenigsquelle.com

For over 25 years, this convivial restaurant has been run by the same team. They serve alpine food. Try their schnitzels! Or ask what's on the handwritten menu that changes daily. You won't be disappointed. In summer, you can sit outside underneath the old trees.

89 STEREO CAFE

**Residenzstrasse 25
Altstadt-Lehel ①
+49 (0)89 242 101 43
*stereo-cafe.de***

Located on the first floor above a menswear shop, this cafe has a large studio window at the front and a hidden sun deck at the rear. They serve homemade cakes as well as lunch specials and a selection of aperitifs and liquor.

90 CAFÉ STOCKHOLM

**Lämmerstrasse 6
Ludwigsvorstadt ①
+49 (0)151 433 512 11**

This cafe is so atypical of Munich that it really is a pleasure to stop here. The Swedish owner cooks the craziest dishes, the decor is reminiscent of a beach bar and the general attitude is one of mad freedom. Enjoy!

90 CAFÉ STOCKHOLM

DIOS MINGA

55 PLACES FOR A DRINK

The 5 best places to
SAMPLE SOME BEER

---

91 MÜNCHEN 72
Holzstrasse 16
Isarvorstadt ②
+49 (0)89 973 437 85
muenchen72.de

This unpretentious bar's name refers to the 1972 Olympics, which took place in Munich, as you can tell from the bar's design. The team always comes up with something new, the menu is adapted to the seasons and popular with the locals. In summer you can also sit outside.

92 SCHELLING-SALON
Schellingstrasse 54
Maxvorstadt ③
+49 (0)89 272 0788
schelling-salon.de

Many generations have sat here at the wooden tables or played a game of pool. This place is unique in many ways: the truly traditional feel of it, the stories and the memories, the fact that you can play pool and table tennis. Once you've been there, you'll understand why so many people call it their second living room.

93 SUBSTANZ
Ruppertstrasse 28
Isarvorstadt ②
+49 (0)89 721 2749
substanz-club.de

The Substanz always had a down-to-earth way of saying "Each to their own". Their recipe for success: a bit of punk with a bit of anarchy, some live music and subculture thrown in for good measure. Enjoy some normal-priced beer and the unconventional audience, watch a game or play a game of foosball.

94 KLENZE 17

Klenzestrasse 17
Isarvorstadt ②
+49 (0)89 255 442 77
klenze17.de

A nice pub for a beer with friends. They also serve traditional pub food such as schnitzel, burgers or chili con carne. Everything is as it should be: unchanged, like an old friend that you visit from time to time. In the back room you can watch football matches.

95 TUMULT

Blütenstrasse 4
Maxvorstadt ③
+49 (0)89 273 724 63
tumult-in-muenchen.de

Could there really be a bar like this one in the middle of this swanky neighbourhood? The pub is in a basement, the people here know their way around beer and they play punk, ska and rock music. Either you like it – depending on if this is your sort of thing – or you don't.

92 SCHELLING-SALON

5 renowned
WINE BARS and
WINE SHOPS

96 **GARIBALDI**
Schellingstrasse 60
Maxvorstadt ③
+49 (0)89 272 0906
garibaldi.de

This shop sells fine wines, spirits and food, (mostly) from Italy. Wine is an important aspect of human culture here. Check out their counter with Italian *alimentari* and, if you really don't feel like having a good glass of wine, then order an espresso.

97 **225 LITER**
Pariser Strasse 17
Au-Haidhausen ⑤
+49 (0)89 513 046 44
225liter.de

The owners search for small and rather unknown winemakers, who are very passionate about their wine. Everyone is welcome here, whether you are a wine connoisseur or completely clueless about wine. They organise a wine tasting (at a small charge) every Friday from 5 pm at the back of the shop.

98 **DIOS MINGA**
Thalkirchner Str. 11
Isarvorstadt ②
+49 (0)89 216 682 72
diosminga.de

A combination of a wine bar and a small restaurant: where you can eat Iberian and Bavarian specialities, drink wines from Spain and Portugal and spend a relaxed evening in a pleasant atmosphere. It's like a mini vacation.

99 **VINTAGE SELECTION**

Marienstrasse 18
Altstadt-Lehel ①
+49 (0)89 255 460 61
vintage-selection.de

This wine bar offers wine lovers a comprehensive overview of Germany's wine landscape. They always look for what they call the best pleasure for money. Trust them – and savour the wine!

100 **SÜDHANG SENDLING**

Valleystrasse 42
Sendling ⑥
+49 (0)178 899 9499
suedhang-sendling.de

You'd be hard pushed to find a more relaxed place to drink wine in Munich. The owners turned parts of their apartment into this cosy wine shop. They also offer Korean bar food such as *gimbab* (Korea's answer to sushi) or *kimchi*. What a mix! Please note that they close at 8 pm.

98 DIOS MINGA

5

TEAHOUSES

to relax

---

101 TUSHITA
Klenzestrasse 53
Isarvorstadt ②
+49 (0)89 548 432 39
tushita.eu

This teashop is the perfect place to warm up on a cold day and enjoy a vegan cake along with a cup of tea. It's all about creating a superb experience. Here tea is still served in the traditional way. They also have a daily vegan special.

102 THE VICTORIAN HOUSE
Frauenstrasse 14
Altstadt-Lehel ①
+49 (0)89 255 469 47
victorianhouse.de

Are you an Anglophile or are you just pining for a traditional afternoon tea with scones and clotted cream? Look no further. The Victorian House serves sweet treats, you are surrounded by antiques, and you will definitely find someone to discuss Brexit.

103 LETCHA: ORGANIC TEA ROOM
Herzogstrasse 1-A
Schwabing ④
letcha.de

At Letcha, you'll find all kinds of different organic teas with special toppings. The tea is lovingly and elaborately prepared in front of you. The tearoom specialises in matcha drinks and also serves some matcha cakes and Asian patisserie. A refreshing stop!

104 MANDARIN ORIENTAL-THE LOUNGE

Neuturmstrasse 1
Altstadt-Lehel ①
+49 (0)89 290 988 29
mandarinoriental.de

At the five-star Mandarin Oriental, you can enjoy afternoon tea in an upscale atmosphere, even if you're not a hotel guest. Pay The Lounge a visit and enjoy the international flair and the high quality of everything they serve. Locals come here too.

105 LAIFUFU TEESALON

Maillingerstrasse 14
Neuhausen-
Nymphenburg ⑦
+49 (0)89 550 699 88
laifufu.de

In addition to Munich's most exquisite selection of oolong teas, the Laifufu tearoom also offers other carefully selected teas. The owner organises Taiwan-style tea ceremonies (not as meditative as elsewhere; the emphasis is on the pleasure of drinking tea). Tea ceremonies must be booked in advance and take place on Saturdays.

5 cosy places to
SIT OUTSIDE

---

106 CAFÉ IN DER GLYPTOTHEK

Königsplatz 3
Maxvorstadt ③
+49 (0)89 288 083 80
antike-am-
koenigsplatz.mwn.de

The Glyptothek has been written up in many a tourist guide, so let's just skip that bit here. The cafe inside however is highly recommended because it is so peaceful even though it is in the centre of the city. The Glyptothek has a courtyard, where you can sit in summer.

107 STADTCAFÉ

Sankt-Jakobs-Platz 1
Altstadt-Lehel ①
+49 (0)89 266 949
stadtcafe-muenchen.de

This cafe was regarded as the meeting place of Munich's intellectuals for many years. While the tourists sit out front in the square, most locals prefer the shade of the charming courtyard. Either way, it's always a good choice.

108 KANTINE KIOSK AKADEMIE DER BILDENDEN KÜNSTE

Akademiestrasse 2-4
Maxvorstadt ③
+49 (0)89 552 975 15

You really should explore the neighbourhood around the Academy of Fine Arts. Young artists, older professors and great architecture! And in the middle of all that: a canteen that is open to the public, with lots of glass and a great outdoor terrace in front of the building. Self-service. Order cakes, snacks and a hot meal from the counter.

109 BOB IM PARK

Olympiapark
München
Milbertshofen ④
+49 (0)89 726 692 22
cafe-kubitscheck.de/
bob-im-park

Olympic flair and student life. This cafe is located on the tennis and beach volleyball facilities of the Technical University (you do not have to be a student to play here). They serve delicious cakes during the day, and in the evenings, guests can bring barbecue food and grill it on-site for a small fee. Only open during the summer months.

110 CAFÉ GANS AM WASSER

Siegenburger Str. 41
Sendling ⑥
gansamwasser.de

This looks like an enchanted fairy-tale park, with tents, garlands and umbrellas and food and drinks that you can order from the old trailer. The cafe is located on a lake in the park in lush green surroundings. Sometimes they also organise cultural events here.

107 STADTCAFÉ

5 charming traditional
COFFEE HOUSES

---

111 CAFÉ KREUTZKAMM
Maffeistrasse 4
Altstadt-Lehel ①
+49 (0)89 293 277
kreutzkamm.de

A cafe with a dignified atmosphere and a long-standing tradition. Be sure to try the *Baumkuchen*, you'll rarely find them anywhere else. Or the so-called men's cake which has many fans of all ages. There are even online discussions about how best to crack the chocolate coating.

112 MARAIS
Parkstrasse 2
Schwanthaler-
höhe ⑥
+49 (0)89 500 945 52
cafe-marais.de

An old clothing store that has been transformed into something very special. The Marais is not just a cafe, but also a shop that sells furniture, jewellery, scarves, hats and organic cosmetics. Some of the tables are in the former shop windows. A rather unusual start to your day in Munich.

113 BAR CENTRALE
Ledererstrasse 23
Altstadt-Lehel ①
+49 (0)89 223 762
bar-centrale.com

Fans of Italy get their money's worth here. You can sit in the back room, but the front area resembles a bar in an Italian square in every possible sense. Friendly staff, good cappuccino – what more could you ask for?

114 CAFE FRISCHHUT

Prälat-Zistl-Strasse 8
Altstadt-Lehel ①
+49 (0)89 260 231 56

Different types of delicious Bavarian fried pastries, which are freshly prepared in front of you. The cafe has stayed true to itself and is distinctly unimpressed by the chichi places around it. You'll soon realise that many guests have been coming here for several decades for the good quality.

115 CAFE JASMIN

Steinheilstrasse 20
Maxvorstadt ③
+49 (0)89 452 274 06
cafe-jasmin.com

The old Cafe Jasmin with its upholstered furniture and fifties flair has been taken over by a youngish crew, which runs it now. It looks like your grandma's home, but the audience is younger and the food is more contemporary. Open until 1 am, so you can move smoothly from cakes to cocktails, if you find it difficult to leave.

112 MARAIS

5 of the most
BEAUTIFUL CAFES

---

116 CAFÉ EDELWEISS
Sankt-Martin-Str. 9
Obergiesing ⑧
+49 (0)89 547 811 61
edel-weiss.info

What an interesting interior this cafe has! Is it simple or sophisticated? You'll have to decide that for yourself. It is definitely worth seeing, and they also have some very good cakes and surprisingly cheap drinks. Well worth it, in any event.

117 MAX2
Maximilianstrasse 42
Altstadt-Lehel ①
+49 (0)89 189 269 77
cafe-max2.de

Max2 is located in an impressive building, namely the Ethnological Museum, which is also worth seeing. You can have lunch or an Aperol under the arcades. The food is cooked on the spot and healthy. You'll definitively have a good time here.

118 KAFFEERÖSTEREI VOGELMAIER
Einsteinstrasse 125
Au-Haidhausen ⑤
+49 (0)89 237 470 50
vogelmaier.de

Two people who have turned their passion into their job, running a cafe and coffee roastery, roasting speciality coffees from fair trade beans. Their slow-roasted coffee tastes particularly good in their nice, laidback cafe.

119 **BELLEVUE DI MONACO**
Müllerstrasse 2-6
Isarvorstadt ②
+49 (0)89 550 577 50
bellevuedimonaco.de

The story of this cafe is too long to be told here. But it is a good one! Enjoy the coffee and find out where you've ended up. This place is like a history of Munich and its inhabitants.

120 **CAFE LOTTI**
Schleissheimer Strasse 13
Maxvorstadt ③
+49 (0)89 615 191 97
cafe-lotti.lotti-muenchen.de

When a girl's dream becomes a cafe, with pink walls and chandeliers, a little feel-good oasis with plenty of treats. The team wants to add a silver lining to everyone's day and they really do. Many people swear that the pancakes are the best in town.

116 **CAFÉ EDELWEISS**

5 fabulous
ROOFTOP BARS

―――

121 HOUSETOP-BAR (LOVELACE)

Kardinal-Faulhaber-
Strasse 1
Altstadt-Lehel ①
+49 (0)89 215 407 90
thelovelace.com

One of the city's hottest hot spots, a hip mix of a hotel, club culture and more. Take the lift to the top floor where you'll find the Housetop bar, with its green wall living plants. On the opposite corner there's a door to the terrace. Climb up the stairs for an amazing view over the roofs of Munich.

122 VORHOELZER FORUM: CAFÉ

Arcisstrasse 21,
Raum 5170
Maxvorstadt ③
+49 (0)163 152 4758
ar.tum.de/vf/startseite

Not very easy to find but boy, is it worth it! Turn left at the main entrance of this university building, there is a lift at the end of the long corridor. Go to the fifth floor where heaven awaits you. A bright room for the cafe, behind which the spacious roof terrace opens up in front of you. Enjoy the fantastic views!

123 MS UTTING

Lagerhausstrasse 5
Sendling ⑥

This is an actual ship on a bridge. Yes, that's right. The ship opened its doors in 2018, offering an interesting mix of culture and good food. Everyone in Munich wants to check out this place, so you will have to exercise some patience.

124 **EMIKO ROOF TOP TERRACE**
Viktualienmarkt 6
Altstadt-Lehel ①
+49 (0)89 4111908111
louis-hotel.com/
emiko-restaurant-bar

This hotel operates a rooftop bar in summertime, providing a truly stylish and cosy space to spend a nice evening, with great lighting and beautiful parasols. They'll spoil you with high-class Japanese cuisine and Asian-inspired summer cocktails.

125 **FLUSHING MEADOWS**
Fraunhoferstrasse 32
Isarvorstadt ②
+49 (0)89 552 791 70
flushingmeadowshotel.
com

This bar is located on the hotel's top floor. Take the lift to the fourth floor and enjoy the sunny terrace and panoramic view (you might even spot the Zugspitze). They serve aperitifs and cocktails and the staff are really friendly.

123 MS UTTING

5 places to start your
PUB CRAWL

---

126 FRAU BARTELS

Klenzestrasse 51
Isarvorstadt ②
+49 (0)89 997 305 68
fraubartels.de

A bar for everyone, including students, which makes for a good mix of people. Funny furniture, interesting materials. The back room is especially cosy with its leather couch and rugs.

127 COOPERATIVA

Jahnstrasse 35
Isarvorstadt ②
+49 (0)89 202 076 20
cooperativa.de

A vibrant neighbourhood restaurant, where you sit on wooden benches and eat Mediterranean food. The big salads are a popular option. Rather unusual for Munich. You can't book a table and the waiters fill vacant seats with strangers so you get to meet new people. Oh, and cash only.

128 CAFE KOSMOS

Dachauer Strasse 7
Maxvorstadt ③
+49 (0)89 552 958 67
cafe-kosmos.de

One of the best bars in the city according to many locals. If you like a packed loud bar, then you'll love this place. Everyone is respectful and nice so you'll feel at home right away. The unrenovated rooms look like they've always been waiting for you. No admission during the Oktoberfest if you are wearing a Bavarian costume.

129 SCHNELLE LIEBE

Thalkirchner Str. 12
Isarvorstadt ②
+49 (0)89 215 787 52

A younger crowd meets in this small and noisy bar to either have a burger before going out or a burger because they are feeling peckish as the night continues. Or they just stop in for a few drinks. Friendly ambience, mixed audience, upbeat atmosphere.

130 UNTER DECK

Oberanger 26
Altstadt-Lehel ①
+49 (0)89 242 937 11

This bar is located in a rather sterile area of the city and has a bit of a sea theme going on. It's groovier and rougher than its surroundings, which is nice. From time to time they host live gigs.

128 CAFE KOSMOS

The 5 most classy
COCKTAIL BARS

---

131 ROOSEVELT
Thierschplatz 5
Altstadt-Lehel ①
+49 (0)89 215 783 00
roosevelt.de

A completely relaxed, classic American bar. They pride themselves on their incredible selection of fine rum. Drinks and cocktails mixed with panache by the barman. A nice neighbourly feel.

132 BRUCKMANN'S
Neureutherstrasse 21
Maxvorstadt ③
+49 (0)89 237 927 72
bruckmanns.bar

This bar is well hidden on a quiet side street. A cosy place for a fun evening. The drinks are fantastic, you can enjoy a few special snacks too. A place for adults in their thirties and forties, to drink and party and enjoy the nightlife. If you turn up early, you can sit outside for a while.

133 SALON PITZELBERGER
Gärtnerplatz 3
Isarvorstadt ②
+49 (0)176 251 984 65
salon-pitzelberger.de

The Gärtnerplatztheater and its recently-opened cellar bar, is located in the centre of the hip Glockenbachviertel. DJs play sets here and the theatre audience mixes with night owls. A bit sophisticated but still very cosy.

134 GOLDENE BAR

Prinzregentenstr. 1
Altstadt-Lehel ①
+49 (0)89 548 047 77
goldenebar.de

A must visit. Sit inside, among the gold and mahogany and the warm lighting or outside, on the spacious terrace. Either way you'll love it. It's part of Haus der Kunst. After 8 pm, you must enter via the terrace at the back of the museum.

135 KONGRESSBAR

Theresienhöhe 15
Schwanthaler-
höhe ⑥
+49 (0)89 452 11 700
kongressbar.de

The 1950s are alive and kicking. Elegant wood panelling, perfectly designed fifties furniture and discreet jazz music in the background create a relaxed and stylish ambience. Once upon a time the bar was part of the city's convention centre. Today, this time capsule lives on.

133 SALON PITZELBERGER

5 bars for
MORE THAN A DRINK

---

136 PIGALLE

Thalkirchner Str. 23
Isarvorstadt ②
+49 (0)172 793 0682
pigalle-münchen.de

Spend an evening in a former table dance bar. The interior hasn't changed a bit, Pigalle still has a lot of plush red velvet, very little light and a pole in the mirrored corner. Just a scenic backdrop for a bar that draws a young and party-friendly crowd.

137 SEHNSUCHT

Amalienstrasse 26
Maxvorstadt ③
+49 (0)89 287 550 88
bar-sehnsucht.de

A stylised bikers' bar that has been lovingly decorated and is run with a lot of dedication. Definitely worth a visit. Don't forget to enquire why there are so many bras hanging above the bar.

138 HOLY HOME

Reichenbachstrasse 21
Isarvorstadt ②
+49 (0)89 201 4546

On weekends, this bar is usually quite packed with young people, who are keen to party. If you arrive early enough, you'll find a seat at one of the large wooden tables which you share with other guests. Don't be intimidated by the monumental alcohol cabinet made out of dark wood and enjoy a good night out on the town.

139 GORILLA BAR

Hirschbergstrasse 23
Neuhausen-
Nymphenburg ⑦
+49 (0)89 978 963 10
gorilla-bar.com

Bars are rare in this part of town, but this one is really chill and fun. Gorilla's staff are doing a good job but they don't take life too seriously. Here you can have a fun evening, you'll be treated kindly and, if you want to, you'll probably end up getting to know the people next to you.

140 VALENTIN STÜBERL

Dreimühlenstrasse 28
Isarvorstadt ②
+49 (0)89 767 570 58
valentinstueberl.com

A pub, where you can drink one or more beers while listening to the DJs. It's unpretentious, a little bit cool and very down to earth. It's one of those places you might fall in love with and want to take home with you. Again, not really around the corner but worth the walk.

138 HOLY HOME

5 great
MUSIC BARS

---

141 IMPORT EXPORT
Dachauer Strasse 114
Schwabing ④
+49 (0)89 726 692 22
import-export.cc

This site is rather rare in a city where property prices are exploding and space is scarce. An alternative cultural scene has developed on this former military site, including this mix of a bar and venue called Import Export. In the near future, the terrain will be 'developed'. So go ahead and attend one of their great live concerts before it's too late.

142 FAVORIT BAR
Damenstiftstrasse 12
Altstadt-Lehel ①

This bar in the city centre is a gem. The walls are mostly unpainted, there is no decoration. The audience is trendy and of all ages. Members of Munich's cultural scene like to meet here. Many of them have known each other for years. You wouldn't bump into this bar by chance, it's too quiet, and too far away from everything.

143 DOWNTOWN
Theklastrasse 1
Isarvorstadt ②
downtownmunich.de

This club plays rap, rhythm-and-blues, dancehall, funk and soul. Located in a basement on a side street, you should turn up before 2 am to avoid long queues.

144 HELENE CLUB

Occamstrasse 5
Schwabing ④
+49 (0)89 740 352 09
helene-liebt-dich.de

A club in the basement of the Helene restaurant. They play pop and rock music classics for anyone who wants to have a fun night out. And it's not just people in their twenties who are singing along and longing for the good old times in Schwabing.

145 HIDE OUT

Volkartstrasse 22
Neuhausen-
Nymphenburg ⑦
+49 (0)89 169 668
hideout-muenchen.de

A good spot for a late-night drink. Many live gigs here – unplugged jazz and blues – so you can chat through the night while listening to some good music.
The bar is in the basement, don't get put off by that. Definitely worth a visit.

MEDICAL ART & MORE

90 PLACES TO SHOP

———

5 magnificent
FLOWER SHOPS

146 FLEUR FATALE

Rumfordstrasse 33
Isarvorstadt ②
+49 (0)89 232 315 51
fleurfatale.de

This elegant flower shop is rather unusual in many ways. The store is quite spacious, with an array of magnificent arrangements. Secondly, they combine traditional floristry with rather extra-ordinary fantasy flowers made of silk. And thirdly, only your nose will be able to tell the difference between the real flowers and the imitations.

147 HERR WISMAYER FÜR BLUMEN

Pilgersheimerstr. 51
Untergiesing-
Harlaching ⑧
+49 (0)89 624 217 85
herrwismayer.
weebly.com

A beautiful flower shop. The owner finds the overall impression his shop makes just as important as every single flower in it. He creates special seasonal exhibits, that are definitely worth seeing.

148 BELFLAIR

Simon-Knoll-Platz 1
Au-Haidhausen ⑤
+49 (0)89 441 195 12
belflair.de

This flower shop is known for its fancy decorations and the high quality of their cut flowers. He receives fresh daily deliveries, mainly from fair trade sources.

149 BLUMEN ADLER

Nymphenburger-
strasse 187
Neuhausen-
Nymphenburg ⑦
+49 (0)89 161 251
blumenadler.de

One of Munich's oldest florists. They work with regional nurseries and pay attention to the origin of the flowers, which are preferably from sustainable and organic sources. A good shop for both traditional and modern bouquets.

150 BLÜTENREIN

Viktualien-
markt III/3
Altstadt-Lehel ①
+49 (0)89 230 767 67
bluetenrein.net

A green oasis in the heart of Viktualien-markt. The stall – and even its roof – is heaving under the many small and large plants! Don't forget to look up at the small circular temple made of ivy, that floats above everything else. Open seven days a week, from 8 am to 6 pm.

150 BLÜTENREIN

The 5 best places to shop for
SOUVENIRS

151 BIERVANA

Hohenzollern-
strasse 61
Schwabing ④
+49 (0)89 200 777 64
biervana.eu

Most visitors associate beer with Munich. So if you're interested in bringing home a hoppy treat, then visit the craft beer centre. The explosion in the craft beer market, including in Bavaria, is like a breath of fresh air in the world of beer.

152 DIE BONBON MANUFAKTUR MÜNCHEN

Kaufingerstrasse 9
Altstadt-Lehel ①
+49 (0)89 255 465 55
dbbmm.de

Munich's first modern candy manufactory produces traditional handmade sweets while you look on. On any given Saturday, there may be as many as 30 people outside the shop. They use antique, traditional moulds. As these are no longer produced, the owner was really happy to get hold of some.

153 KRÄUTERPARADIES LINDIG

Blumenstrasse 15
Altstadt-Lehel ②
+49 (0)89 265 726
phytofit.de

This shop has been selling herbs and natural remedies for over 130 years, with more than 500 different herbs and spices contained in the large wooden drums. All the items have been tested for harmful substances. They also have a good selection of natural oils and a tea for when you are suffering from a head cold.

154 BRAUSESCHWEIN

Frundsberg-
strasse 52
Neuhausen-
Nymphenburg ⑦
+49 (0)89 139 581 12
brauseschwein.de

A very special children's store selling all kinds of nostalgic toys, such as wooden toys, dolls and many other fun and exciting gifts for children. They also have a nice selection of special sweets and joke and tricks that will immediately transport you back to childhood. So yes, this is the place to go, if you want to make your child – and yourself – happy.

155 SERVUS.HEIMAT

Im Tal 20
Altstadt-Lehel ①
+49 (0)89 210 198 15
servusheimat.com/im-
tal-radlsteg

This shop sells a nice selection of lovingly-selected souvenirs. Everything is somehow linked to the alpine and Southern German region with useful little items and funny gifts such as 'weather houses' or whacky cuckoo clocks. An anti-souvenir shop, really, where locals also like to shop.

152 DIE BONBON MANUFAKTUR MÜNCHEN

5 great shops for
MODERN PORCELAIN

156 ANNIKA SCHÜLER
Schraudolph-
strasse 10
Maxvorstadt ③
+49 (0)89 716 960 56
annikaschueler.de

Traditional craftmanship meets contemporary design. Annika Schüler creates handcrafted sleek designs with lovely shapes. She has created a range of functional wares, which help transform the ordinary into something special. A unique fresh, bold and sometimes cheeky take on tradition.

157 NYMPHENBURGER PORZELLAN
Nördliches
Schlossrondell 8
Neuhausen-
Nymphenburg ⑦
+49 (0)89 179 1970
nymphenburg.com

This porcelain is produced in a time capsule. The manufactory is located in a subsidiary building of Nymphenburg Palace, and everything is done according to tradition. They use water power for the potter's wheels and all the pieces are hand-painted. They regularly collaborate with different contemporary artists.

158 DRIN UND DRAN
Steinheilstrasse 12
Maxvorstadt ③
+49 (0)89 542 442 29
drindran.de

A shop on a quiet corner, which produces and sells porcelain and jewellery. Each item is unique. You can watch the designer craft dishes and vessels of timeless and simple beauty, made of the finest and translucent English porcelain. She shares the space with a goldsmith.

159 1260 GRAD PETRA FISCHER

Sedanstrasse 27
Au-Haidhausen ⑤
+49 (0)89 447 706 88
1260grad.de

This ceramics store is both a workshop and a shop. 1260 Grad (degrees) is named after the temperature of the kiln during the firing process. The owner Petra Fischer sells her own stoneware and porcelain designs as well as a selection of other items for a well-laid table.

160 ROSENTHAL

Kardinal-Faulhaber-
Strasse 5
Altstadt-Lehel ①
+49 (0)89 222 617
rosenthal.de

Rosenthal has been producing porcelain in Franconia for 135 years. Nowadays they also cooperate with contemporary artists and designers, selling interior design collections as well as porcelain. Current colour and interior design trends, plus a pop-up flower stall can be found on the first floor. Their concept kitchen is on the second floor.

160 ROSENTHAL

5 of the most
CURIOUS SHOPS

161 **MEDICAL ART & MORE**

Sedanstrasse 29
Au-Haidhausen ⑤
+49 (0)89 260 105 25
medicalartandmore.de

The owner is a medical illustrator. She works on assignments in her shop, while also selling fun, bizarre and high-quality medicine-themed products including anatomical models, as well as the craziest gimmicks like skull bakeware, eye erasers, and a porcelain vessel resembling a brain.

162 **ARIANE LAUE KUNSTHANDEL – RAUM FÜR OBJEKTE**

Theresienstrasse 33
Maxvorstadt ③
+49 (0)89 280 0972
arianelaue.de

'A space for objects'. The translation of the shop's name says it all. This art shop specialises in handicraft treasures up to the 19th century. Ariane Laue is an interior designer, and likes to stage her selection of objects, establishing unusual relationships between them.

163 **ZAUBERFLÖTE**

Falkenturmstrasse 8
Altstadt-Lehel ①
+49 (0)89 225 125

Fans of classical music as well as opera addicts both love this small, well-hidden Munich institution. The owner specialises in rare and special classical music recordings and is always on hand to help you with excellent advice. A good place to discover new gems.

164 DIE RITTER

Thalkirchner Str. 14
Isarvorstadt ②
+49 (0)89 260 117 41
die-ritter.de

Fans of medieval times flock to this shop for advice on swords, epées, daggers, axes, helmets or chain armour. They also sell many other special items, such as objects made of pewter, chess pieces, fantasy figures or custom-made medieval-style jewellery.

165 ARTS IN FABRICS

Fürstenstrasse 6
Maxvorstadt ③
+49 (0)89 200 611 07
artsinfabrics.com

This exceptional fabric shop sells fine Italian designer fabrics, extravagant trims, amazing curtains, exquisite silk and cashmere, fancy brocade and lovely cotton fabrics. Everything looks neat and bright. If textiles are your thing, then this is the place for you.

162 ARIANE LAUE KUNSTHANDEL

The 5 best
FLEA MARKETS

---

166 MIDNIGHT BAZAR
Various addresses
+49 (0)89 516 649 52
midnightbazar.de

This company organises various flea market events that are very popular with the locals. These include a late-night flea market (including some street food stalls), a children's flea market, a 'fashion session' for women, a general fashion flea market called 'Munich Super Sale' and the 'Hall of Taste', with food and groceries. The dates and places change so check their website.

167 OLYMPIAPARK FLOHMARKT PARKHARFE
Schwabing ④
brk-muenchen.de/
aktuelles/aktionen-
veranstaltungen/
rotkreuz-flohmaerkte/
flohmarkt-olympiapark

Hundreds of flea market fans regularly rummage through the bins and haggle in the parking lot (called *Parkharfe*) of the Olympic Park. Usually on Friday and Saturday, unless it's a holiday or a major event. It's one of the city's biggest flea markets with professional dealers as well as occasional sellers.

168 THERESIENWIESEN-FLOHMARKT

Schwanthaler-höhe ⑥
brk-muenchen.de/
aktuelles/aktionen-
veranstaltungen/
rotkreuz-flohmaerkte/
flohmarkt-
theresienwiese

Theresienwiese is the event space of the Oktoberfest. But once a year, the space also becomes a huge flea with 3000 booths attracting 30.000 visitors. The market officially opens at 6 am, but the real 'early birds' come the evening before to secure the best spaces and deals. If you've seen enough, then move on to the Spring Festival (Oktoberfest's little sister) right next to the market.

169 HINTERHOF-FLOHMÄRKTE

Various addresses
hofflohmaerkte.de/
muenchen

On most Saturdays from May to September, people in a given neighbourhood organise yard sales, selling stuff they no longer need. It's a great opportunity to see private gardens you ordinarily wouldn't have access to while bargain hunting. Check the website which lists the dates and neighbourhoods. An excellent and adventurous way to explore the city on foot.

170 FLOHPALAST

Theresienstrasse 81
Maxvorstadt ③
+49 (0)89 218 920 00
flohpalast.de

If there is no flea market when you need one, you can go to a flea market shop. Anyone can rent a shelf here and sell their stuff. The owner is in charge of the sale, during the usual opening hours.

5 shops for
ART MATERIALS,
PAPER & PRINTS

171 CARTA PURA

Schellingstrasse 71
Maxvorstadt ③
+49 (0)89 288 1130
cartapura.de

A nice selection of stationery, bookbinding supplies and above all, special types of paper, such as Japanese paper or Italian Carta Varese. It is also the flagship store of Carta Pura. Whether you are looking for a calendar, boxes or photo albums, everything is perfectly designed with a certain understatement.

172 KARIN TRAXLER

Theresienstrasse 65 –
rear building
Maxvorstadt ③
+49 (0)89 202 441 40
vierwerkstaetten.de

The artist creates the best things out of paper. In addition to paper art and all bookbinding, she produces square and round boxes, trays or drawer cabinets. Her studio is located in an interesting building, where several other artists have their workspaces.

173 KOKOLORES

Wörthstrasse 8
Au-Haidhausen ⑤
+49 (0)89 448 3251
kokolores-muenchen.de

A true paradise for explorers, where you'll find postcards and stationery, as well as beautiful, extraordinary gifts. There's something to everyone's liking here, including fun objects like *Vogelpfeiferl* or beautiful stamps and flipbooks.

174 PS PAPIER

Kaiserstrasse 46
Schwabing ④
+49 (0)89 341 287

Another source for only the finest paper. Elegant notebooks, different types of unique papers, cards and letterheads. They also sell a wide range of writing instruments and stamps. A stylish shop, a special place in a quiet corner of the city.

175 NELLYPAP

Winthirstrasse 10-A
Neuhausen-
Nymphenburg ⑦
+49 (0)89 189 559 77
nellypap.de

The owner is passionate about paper, can you tell? This store sells special cards, wrapping paper, storage boxes, notebooks, stationery and many other fancy and high-quality paper products as well as some stylish handbags.

171 CARTA PURA

5

LIQUOR SHOPS

176 MIKE'S WHISKEY HANDEL

Tal 42
Altstadt-Lehel ①
+49 (0)89 296 389
mikes-whiskeyhandel.
de

There's a bar on the first floor of this lamp shop, or, to be more specific, the training rooms of the American Whiskey Academy. Walk through the sales rooms with the lamps and chandeliers to the saloon. Their evening tastings beneath the chandeliers are legendary. Book in advance.

177 SZENEDRINKS

Fraunhoferstrasse 12
Isarvorstadt ②
+49 (0)89 189 853 33
szenedrink.eu

A stylish shop selling a selection of fine gins, vodkas, schnapps and liqueurs as well as the ingredients to mix them. They also give great advice. Tip: You can buy the *Windspiel* spirits here.

178 VOGELWILDES

Sattlerstrasse 1
Altstadt-Lehel ①
+49 (0)89 210 221 42
vogelwildes-muc.de

A colourful mix of silver jewellery, spirits, leather clothing, bags, all kinds of gifts and many other extraordinary objects. All in a very unusual atmosphere, especially for Munich. Their rather untranslatable name means something like '*tohuwabohuesque*'.

179 COLLECTOR'S CORNER

Augustenstrasse 39
Maxvorstadt ③
+49 (0)89 520 591 45
collectors-corner-
muenchen.de

Buy fine whiskies, rums, gins, vodkas and wines in a listed Ottoman-style interior. In 1866, the store was the headquarters of Bavaria's first cigarette factory and you can still buy exquisite Cuban cigars here today.

180 PACHMAYR

Theresienstrasse 33
Maxvorstadt ③
+49 (0)89 282 102
pachmayr.de

One of Germany's oldest beverage wholesalers still owns its original premises in bustling Maxvorstadt. This traditional company has been handed down from father to son for five generations. They sell an amazing selection of drinks and spirits – some 2000 products – as well as their own gin.

176 MIKE'S WHISKEY HANDEL

5 *wonderful*
BOOKSHOPS

---

181 SODA BOOKS

Rumfordstrasse 3
Isarvorstadt ②
+49 (0)89 202 453 53
sodabooks.com

This store offers the most comprehensive range of national and international magazines and design books (graphics and industry), food and fashion magazines. Unlike other shops, they arrange the magazine covers like in a gallery. All in all a very inspiring collection.

182 L. WERNER

Türkenstrasse 30
Maxvorstadt ③
+49 (0)89 280 544 8
buchhandlung-werner.de

Founded in 1878, this bookstore specialises in architecture and the arts, including photography. The shop is located opposite the Brandhorst Collection. Browse their shelves and feel free to check out the Munich architecture gallery at the rear of the shop, which can be accessed through a back door.

183 BUCHHANDLUNG PERTHEL – BUCHHANDLUNG AM GASTEIG

Rosenheimer Str. 12
Au-Haidhausen ⑤
+49 (0)89 458 799 09
buchperthel.de

A beautiful old bookshop. There is a harpsichord on the first floor, which the owner only plays when he is alone in the shop. They always carry a good selection of English books, also on Bavarian topics, and they have a range of special and historic postcards for every occasion.

184 COLIBRIS

Leonrodstrasse 19
Neuhausen-
Nymphenburg ⑦
+49 (0)89 169 326
buchhandlung-colibri.
buchhandlung.de

A literary bookshop selling fiction, non-fiction, poetry, classics, graphic novels and children's youth books, as well as travel, cooking, audio books and English literature. CoLibris also has a CD and vinyl music department with rock/pop, jazz, world music and classical music.

185 ANTIQUARIAT HAMMERSTEIN

Türkenstrasse 37
Maxvorstadt ③
+49 (0)89 285 183
antiquariat
hammerstein.de

This antiquarian bookshop has been around for decades. Come here to enjoy the shop's special atmosphere. Old issues of a magazine called *Simplicissimus*, which are always available here, are definitely worth picking up.

181 SODA BOOKS

5

HOMEWARE *and* INTERIOR DESIGN

shops

186 SHU SHU

Neuturmstrasse 2
Altstadt-Lehel ①
+49 (0)89 255 490 61
shushu-munich.com

This concept store specialises in Japanese home accessories, gifts, lifestyle and design wares. Visit their shop in the city centre where they sell stylish furniture as well as beautiful home accessories from Japan. They also have a good gift range.

187 STEIN 11

Steinstrasse 11
Au-Haidhausen ⑤
+49 (0)89 621 891 71
stein11.de

The solid wooden Shaker-style furniture they sell here combines surprisingly well with the modern shelving systems and high-quality accessories. A neat store that is always worth a visit. You might find your favourite piece of furniture here!

188 WEISSGLUT

Hohenzollern-
strasse 8
Schwabing ④
+49 (0)89 388 693 68
weissglut-design.de

A creative couple fulfilled their own personal dream (mostly in white) with this lovingly decorated concept store. They sell a nice selection of home accessories, small pieces of furniture, women's fashion, Scandinavian design furniture, natural cosmetics, jewellery and much more. Always something new to discover here, so pop in often.

189 LADOUG

Müllerstrasse 30,
Eingang: Papa-
Schmid-Strasse
Isarvorstadt ②
+49 (0)89 242 149 90
ladoug.de

This place sells interior decoration from all over the world. Every item is an example of fine craftsmanship. Whether you like old or new, unique or industrial design, you'll always find some inspiration and ideas for your home here. They also sell a line of cashmere designer clothing for women.

190 FREIRAUM

Damenstiftstrasse 4
Altstadt-Lehel ①
+49 (0)89 260 226 55
freiraum-muenchen.de

The team has given much thought to what constitutes good furniture. The individual products are carefully selected, taking into account the quality of workmanship, the quality of handling the object, and the formal quality. Everything they sell should still be attractive in 10 years' time. The loft-like showroom is bright and a lot of fun to go through.

187 STEIN 11

5 up-and-coming
LABELS FROM MUNICH

191 WE.RE

Buttermelcher-
strasse 5
Isarvorstadt ②
werealabel.com

Urban zeitgeist meets high-quality fashion. The designers Katharina Weber and Theresa Reiter create clothing for men and women who prefer a more sophisticated minimalist style. Since 2014, the 'pop-up label' has become the to-go address for androgynous, wearable cool elegance. The studio is in the shop so customers always get to meet the designers.

192 VOR SHOES

Schraudolph-
strasse 10
Maxvorstadt ③
+49 (0)172 847 62 59
vor.shoes

A premium footwear brand, as well as an anti-brand. VOR sells a contemporary and limited range of sneakers. All their shoes are manufactured in Germany. Check their website for retailers in Munich.

193 MY BROTHERHOOD

Görresstrasse 16
Maxvorstadt ③
+49 (0)89 272 45 05

The founder Rick Thepsuwan runs his fashion label out of his mother's travel agency. My Brotherhood creates streetwear and fashion for people, who enjoy life with their loved ones, friends, brothers and sisters and who share the vision that a label can form a community that supports everyone involved.

194 A KIND OF GUISE

Adalbertstrasse 41-B
Maxvorstadt ③
+49 (0)89 726 695 11
akindofguise.com

This beautiful and cosy store is easily overlooked. It is the home of a label that has evolved into an internationally well-reputed brand for timeless and functional, yet witty streetwear. Their wearable quality designs are manufactured in Germany.

195 ME&MAY

Amalienstrasse 55
Maxvorstadt ③
+49 (0)89 954 452 99
meandmay.de

At Me&May you will find the label's latest collection. Combine French charm with German precision and a dash of simple elegance and you get Me&May. The shop also sells matching accessories, small gifts and high-quality bags, purses, belts, jewellery and shoes by various other Munich brands.

The 5 best shops for
VINTAGE CLOTHING

196 VINTAGE LOVE

Frauenstrasse 22
Altstadt-Lehel ①
+49 (0)89 255 422 07
vintageandmore.de

Vintage Love offers a fine collection of ballgowns, evening and cocktail dresses as well as bags, shoes and belts. Immerse yourself in a world of fashion, and be enchanted by the glamour of the fifties, sixties and seventies. You'll truly look like a star and, what is more, at prices you can afford.

197 DIAKONIE BLUTENBURGSTRASSE

Blutenburgstrasse 65
Neuhausen-
Nymphenburg ⑦
+49 (0)89 121 595 27
diakonia-kleidsam.de

A place to shop for chic secondhand women's fashion including high-quality day and evening fashion and exclusive designer clothes, as well as matching accessories such as shoes, bags and jewellery. The church-owned store employs people with disabilities who often have trouble finding a job.

198 EXCLUSIV FIRST-CLASS SECOND HAND

Wurzerstrasse 10
Altstadt-Lehel ①
+49 (0)89 291 601 70
designersecondhand-
muenchen.de

From street-style to elegant, from vintage to avant-garde, from ready-to-wear to haute couture. Here you'll find up-to-date and very exclusive secondhand designer fashions, a selection of collections, unique vintage treasures, from some of the world's hottest labels. They also stock shoes and accessories.

199 FREIE SELBSTHILFE

Theresienstrasse 66
Maxvorstadt ③
+49 (0)89 282 715

Germany's oldest secondhand shop is tucked away in a backyard, between various office spaces. After the war, the impoverished nobility sold their belongings here. Today, 18 lively ladies run the business on a voluntary basis, selling everything from porcelain to paintings and clothes. The clientele is diverse, from widowed men in need of advice on clothing, to students from nearby universities, who stock up on crockery.

200 IKI M.

Adalbertstrasse 45
Maxvorstadt ③
+49 (0)89 954 938 25
iki-m.de

'Vive la bohème' is the motto of this small store, where you'll find a good mix of both vintage and new items. They want to sell clothes based on new ideas, good value and great design and they prefer fair trade and environmentally-friendly products.

5 of the best
SHOPS FOR MEN

201 THE SECOND GERDISMANN

Barer Strasse 74
Maxvorstadt ③
+49 (0)89 809 932 40
thesecond-
gerdismann.de

Let's start with a secondhand option. Here you will find the best designer clothes, shoes and accessories. Everything a man needs, if he wants to dress smartly without breaking the bank. Leaving some money to spend at the other shops in our selection.

202 HANNES ROETHER

Türkenstrasse 94
Maxvorstadt ③
+49 (0)89 189 221 15
hannesroether.de

In 2005, Hannes Roether launched his own menswear label. His philosophy: make clothes, not fashion. For people who are up for modern and casual looks. They also sell a women's collection. Definitely worth a visit.

203 STEREO MUC

Residenzstrasse 25
Altstadt-Lehel ①
+49 (0)89 242 039 54
stereo-muc.de

This cool place is located in the city centre, near the usual flagship stores. They sell quality sportswear, ready-to-wear, accessories and grooming products for men. For men who want to distinguish themselves from the mainstream without chasing trends.

204 HIRMER

Kaufingerstrasse 28
Altstadt-Lehel ①
+49 (0)89 236 830
hirmer.de

While this may look like a classic menswear shop at first glance, it is also very creative and modern upon closer inspection. The company is family-owned and has managed to place itself at the top of the Munich men's clothing business. Hip brands and classic suites. And the salespeople can size you up at a glance.

205 RALF'S FINE GARMENTS

Fraunhoferstrasse 29
Isarvorstadt ②
+49 (0)89 189 527 95
ralfsfinegarments.com

The owner wants to offer beautiful things that cannot be found just anywhere. He knows many of the manufacturers in person, which is why he has such a nice (and limited!) selection. A shop for stylish individualists.

5 fancy
FASHION SHOPS FOR WOMEN

206 ALPENRAUM

Frundsbergstrasse 17
Neuhausen-
Nymphenburg ⑦
+49 (0)89 120 031 66
alpenraum-
muenchen.de

A shop with a great concept. Stop at the stylish coffee bar near the entrance for an espresso after which you can browse their collections of Italian, French and Scandinavian fashion. They also sell basics, as well as special accessories.

207 BEAN STORE

Theresienstrasse 25
Maxvorstadt ③
+49 (0)89 461 334 89
bean-store.de

This place endeavours to sell everything you need to express yourself and to make shopping an adventure. Be inspired by their employees and the special range of brands. A place for beautiful fashion and cool women.

208 WILD MUNICH

Belgradstrasse 5
Schwabing ④
+49 (0)89 462 241 06
wild-munich.com

Trendy looks, top designers and brands. Clothes for all walks of life, from casual and understated to opulent, but never mainstream. They also sell shoes, bags, scarves and home fragrances. A hotspot for fashionistas, trendsetters and especially for women, who like their fashion to reflect their personality.

209 LIEBSCHAFTEN

Herzogstrasse 84
Schwabing ④
+49 (0)89 550 657 40
liebschaften-laden.de

A store with a tasteful selection of clothes. Theirs is a feminine and elegant style, although they also sell more casual and sporty fashions. Here, you'll find a wide range of new trends for everyday situations, with an emphasis on sustainable and fair production.

210 NIA. PRÊT-À-PORTER

Türkenstrasse 35
Maxvorstadt ③
+49 (0)89 286 739 50
nia-carrousel.de

A wide selection of trendy Scandinavian and French brands. The style is feminine with playful skirts, pretty dresses, accessories and much more, for fun looks for every season.

5

CONCEPT STORES

to check out

211 DK STIL
Siegfriedstrasse 11
Schwabing ④
+49 (0)177 299 90 43
dk-stil.de

DK Stil sells lovingly chosen products including jewellery, accessories and cashmere from distant countries, and selected items from Munich. Pieces that are special, but that can be used every day. Quality is a priority.

212 KARUSA
Humboldtstrasse 6
Untergiesing ⑧
+49 (0)89 614 664 24
karusa.de

Shop here for handicrafts, gifts and all kinds of gadgets. The shop sells handmade products as well as some secondhand fashion for women and children.

213 HIER STUDIO
Innere Wiener
Strasse 24
Au-Haidhausen ⑤
hier.studio

Everything here was designed in Munich and much of it has also been produced in the city. A good selection of local design, from stationery and fashion to cosmetics and product design. The shop's design is equally eye-catching.

214 GALORE

Belgradstrasse 47
Schwabing ④
+49 (0)89 973 911 36
storegalore.de

What a surprise package this store is! Selling natural cosmetics, home and interior decoration, backpacks, sunglasses and digital gadgets. What's more, it's also a place to relax. You can just hang around or co-work and the coffee shop sells some nice treats. They also organise seminars at their community table.

215 ABOUT GIVEN

Baaderstrasse 55
Isarvorstadt ②
+49 (0)89 189 128 25
aboutgiven.de

A nice selection of ecological and fair fashion for adults and children (up to seven years). Very fresh, very contemporary. They sell different denim brands and they always give useful advice. Accessories, jewellery, bags and shoes. Many of the products are vegan.

5 stores for custom-designed
JEWELLERY

216 COCII

Corneliusstrasse 12
Isarvorstadt ②
+49 (0)177 491 1114
cocii.de

Cocii is the label of a designer, who sells her jewellery here – sharing the shop with a designer of fabulous bags – and produces it on-site. She draws on tradition to produces timeless pieces. A place to shop for unique and really affordable jewels.

217 ANNE VON WAECHTER

Sedanstrasse 24
Au-Haidhausen ⑤
+49 (0)89 489 1999
annevonwaechter.de

Everything here is completely unique because this jewellery designer combines old and new materials, unique and precious items. Antique silk, cameos or corals are reused and combined with silver, gold or pearls. Everything looks adorable, without being old-fashioned at all.

218 SCHLEGELSCHMUCK

Nordendstrasse 7-A
Maxvorstadt ③
+49 (0)89 271 0071
schlegelschmuck.de

A sleek, very bright store sets the stage for the contemporary art jewellery of this designer and artist. Bold colours are mixed with texture. The colourful pendants are a popular choice. The designer is inspired by music, theatre and art.

219 **PATRIK MUFF**

Ledererstrasse 10
Altstadt-Lehel ①
+49 (0)89 123 7040
patrikmuff.com

Patrik Muff is a contemporary designer and goldsmith, who designs contemporary versions of craft and baroque ornaments. A touch of pomp and punk. Studio Muff has collaborated with several artists and fashion brands like Jenny Holzer, Strellson, Nymphenburg Porcelain or Birkenstock.

220 **CHRISTIANE OEXL**

Türkenstrasse 78,
Rückgebäude
Maxvorstadt ③
+49 (0)89 280 0247
christianeoexl.com

A special location for a special store. The studio of this friendly goldsmith is located at the end of the courtyard, up the stairs. People in the neighbourhood think of her as a confidant and like to come to her for beautiful jewellery or a new ring.

216 COCII

5
MUNICH DESIGNERS
in the spotlight

221 INGO MAURER

Kaiserstrasse 47
Schwabing ④
+49 (0)89 381 606 91
ingo-maurer.com

Ingo Maurer's studio is located in the heart of Schwabing. Their 700-square-metre showroom is huge and definitely worth visiting, with over 100 lighting products, prototypes and individual pieces exhibited in a former production hall. Also a great introduction to the complex process behind creating a design lamp.

222 ANTON DOLL HOLZMANUFAKTUR

Lilienstrasse 3-5
Au-Haidhausen ⑤
+49 (0)89 416 163 660
antondoll.de

Furniture that will give you a lifetime of enjoyment. You can touch and test many of the tables, stools and other solid wood pieces of furniture of this design manufactory in their shop. You will also find new products and prototypes here as well as beautiful home accessories.

223 MAGAZIN

Kardinal-Faulhaber-Strasse 11
Altstadt-Lehel ①
+49 (0)89 238 880 31
magazin.com

A selection of artistic products by renowned manufacturers, plus household items they produce themselves in collaboration with designers. The place is design-heavy, bright and structured. Many of the items fit in your hand luggage.

224 **HOLZRAUSCH**

Corneliusstrasse 2
Isarvorstadt ②
+49 (0)89 189 328 80
holzrausch.de

A gallery, workshop and showroom in one. This is neither a furniture shop, nor a kitchen showroom, but rather an exhibition about the company's strengths, i.e., materials, architecture and design.

225 **VITSOE**

Türkenstrasse 36
Maxvorstadt ③
+49 (0)89 230 770 54
vitsoe.com

Vitsoe's shelves and furniture, which were designed by Dieter Rams in 1960, are among the design world's earliest examples of the 'living better with less, which lasts longer' ethos. Visit their first German store in Theresienstrasse to check out their no-frills designs.

224 **HOLZRAUSCH**

The 5 best
COSTUME SHOPS

226 GOTTSEIDANK

Schleissheimer
Strasse 273
Milbertshofen ④
+49 (0)89 358 999 180
gottseidank.com

Traditional costumes have become a rare sight on Munich's streets unless at the Octoberfest, and even then they're usually the jokey kind. This is where Gottseidank (Thank God) saves the day with beautiful modern *Dirndls*, made out of high-quality fabrics. Men can combine their *Lederhosen* with a woollen hoodie.

227 ALMLIEBE

Ickstattstrasse 22
Isarvorstadt ②
+49 (0)89 552 974 71
almliebe.com

This lovingly designed shop in Glockenbachviertel has a small but good selection of modern costumes for the alpine lifestyle for women, men and more recently also for children, as well as some home accessories. From the casual hooded *Janker* (traditional Bavarian jacket) and the high-end deerskin trousers to the traditional high-necked *Dirndl*. A place that prides itself on tradition and quality.

228 HOLAREIDULIJÖ

Schellingstrasse 81
Maxvorstadt ③
+49 (0)89 271 7745
holareidulijö.com

The best shop for antique and secondhand *Lederhosen,* where they take original Bavarian clothes very seriously. They sell everything here, including *Dirndls*, regional costumes, Bavarian shoes, mountain boots, costume jewellery... Note that this is not a tourist shop.

229 NOH NEE

Steinstrasse 28
Au-Haidhausen ⑤
+49 (0)89 237 992 39
nohnee.com

A mix of the brilliant colours and elaborate designs of African fabrics which are used for traditional Bavarian Dirndl patterns. Every Dirndl à l'Africaine is unique and a tribute to the pride of the woman who wears it. Also check out their small collection of coats, skirts, dresses, blouses and trousers.

230 AMSEL

Adalbertstrasse 14
Maxvorstadt ③
+49 (0)89 200 610 02
amsel-fashion.com

This Munich-based family business designs high-quality women's and men's costumes, as well as alpine fashion, that may look traditional but works equally well today. They combine Bavarian craftsmanship with British flair, calling the result 'British Bavarian'. Each piece is handcrafted in Europe.

5

MUNICH
ENTREPRENEURS

231 LOVE KIDSWEAR

+49 (0)89 767 022 38
love-kidswear.com

This label produces stylish children's clothes for boys and girls up to the age of 14. They use sustainable materials only and work with fairly paid workers in Portugal. Check their website for stores in Munich that stock the label.

232 STUDIO 163

Nymphenburger
Strasse 151
Neuhausen-
Nymphenburg ⑦
+49 (0)89 189 282 67
studio163.de

The place to go for contemporary cashmere knitwear. Designed in Munich, created in a small workshop in Mongolia. The two designers work closely with the wool spinner as well as with the workshop, which employs 15 women.

233 SAINT CLOUDS – I WANT YOU NAKED

saint-clouds.com

Their packaging says: 'I want you naked'. These high-quality natural cosmetics are made with 100% natural ingredients only. The owners wanted to combine the healing powers of plants, salts and oils in products, that appeal to present day customers. Handmade in Munich.

234 BEYER'S OIL

beyersoil.com

Bavarian handmade beard care products. Why not try the local version of beard oil, which is produced near the Alps? All the ingredients are 100% natural, like in their beard balm and shampoo. Check their website for a list of retail stores.

235 JUTELAUNE

jutelaune.com

This young label produces handmade shoes in Spain. The *avarcas* and *espadrilles* are traditional shoes, made by local craftsmen in Menorca and La Rioja. They sell a high-quality product from local artisans in Spain, working with local tradesmen and labour. The result: a simple, stylish and, above all, ethical shoe.

KULTURSTRAND

75 WAYS TO DISCOVER THE SPIRIT OF MUNICH

5 nice and pleasant
BEER GARDENS

236 **WIRTSHAUS AM BAVARIAPARK**

Theresienhöhe 15
Schwanthaler-
höhe ③
+49 (0)89 452 116 91
wirtshaus-am-
bavariapark.com

This beer garden is tucked away right behind the Bavaria statue, just a few metres from Theresienwiese. It looks as if it has been around for quite some time and yet it was only built in 2007. Old chestnut trees provide shade, there is a large self-service area, the food is good. Everything you need to understand the beer garden lifestyle.

237 **MAX-EMANUEL-BRAUEREI**

Adalbertstrasse 33
Maxvorstadt ③
+49 (0)89 271 5158
max-emanuel-
brauerei.de

The beer garden of this former brewery is tucked away in bustling Maxvorstadt, the university quarter. It doesn't offer as much space as other beer gardens, but it's always a good opportunity to sit and chat with the locals next to you.

238 **BIERGARTEN AM MUFFATWERK**

Zellstrasse 4
Au-Haidhausen ⑤
+49 (0)89 458 750 73
muffatwerk.de/en/
pages/biergarten

This beer garden is part of Muffatwerk, a former power plant, which was converted into an important cultural centre. Definitely worth a visit because of its unique location near the River Isar, the late opening hours and the organic food.

239 HOFBRÄUKELLER AM WIENER PLATZ

Innere Wiener Strasse 19
Au-Haidhausen ⑤
+49 (0)89 459 9250
hofbraeukeller.de

A classic, worth seeing. Crunching gravel on the ground, the clinking of steins and above all that, the murmur you hear when many people are out for a beer with their friends at the same time. There is a small children's playground at the back.

240 NOCKERBERG

Hochstrasse 77
Au-Haidhausen ⑤
+49 (0)89 459 9130
paulaner-nockherberg.com

People have been drinking beer here for many years. Both the restaurant and the beer garden reopened in 2018, after a major refurbishment. The old chestnut trees were preserved, so they continue to provide shade in the beer garden which is located above the brewery's historic beer cellars. A nice combination of tradition and innovation.

171 WIRTSHAUS AM BAVARIAPARK

5 *great spots to*
ENJOY THE RIVER ISAR

---

241 KABELSTEG
Altstadt-Lehel ① ⑤

This spot is (not only) popular with families. It is probably the best place to be near the River Isar in the city centre, and, for those who are keen, to take a dip, or even float down a little stretch of it. Please do take care and ask locals for advice. There are plenty of cases of people who have drowned in the Isar! You can buy drinks at the nearby Alpine Museum cafe.

242 FLAUCHERSTANDL
Zentralländ-strasse 35
Thalkirchen ⑥
+49 (0)179 592 5572

This small kiosk is located just south of the Isarauen, the green area around the River Isar. In spite of its name it is not next to Flaucher, but next to Flosslände. In the summer, things get less busy here than in the surrounding area. They sell freshly grilled *Currywurst*, chilled drinks and ice cream. A good place for a picnic by the river.

243 GROSSHESSELOHER BRÜCKE
Untergiesing-Harlaching ⑥

This railway bridge sits high above the river. A combined foot and bike path runs under the tracks. From here, you can enjoy a fantastic view over the valley of the Isar. This is also the city's southern limit.

244 KULTURSTRAND

Auf der Insel
Altstadt-Lehel ⑤
kulturstrand.org

This 'culture beach' takes place from May to August on the Museumsinsel, north of Ludwigsbrücke. It is open daily from 12 to midnight and creates a genuine holiday atmosphere in the heart of the city. In addition to drinks and street food, Kulturstrand is an open cultural platform with lots of different performances and concerts.

245 MARIENKLAUSEN-BRÜCKE

Thalkirchen ⑥

In the recent past, the Isar's river bed has been widened, concrete embankments removed and the banks flattened so the river can reclaim its natural course. This bridge (for pedestrians and cyclists only) is a particularly beautiful place to admire this 'new' Isar.

241 KABELSTEG

The 5 best places for
A BREAK IN THE SUN

---

246 MAX-JOSEPH-PLATZ
Altstadt-Lehel ①

You can sit in the sun on a longish platform on the south side of the Residenz, the palace in the centre of town. There is so much going on, you can watch people as they head into town or to the opera or simply enjoy the moment.

247 KÖNIGSPLATZ
Maxvorstadt ③

The early morning hours are an excellent time to sit on the steps of the Glyptothek and Antikensammlung. As it is slightly sheltered from the wind, it is a great place to enjoy the first rays of sunshine in spring.

248 GÄRTNERPLATZ
Isarvorstadt

Very popular with the young crowd, who enjoy the outdoor atmosphere in one of the most expensive neighbourhoods in Munich. In the evenings, they buy a cold beer in one of the surrounding shops. It's a bit quieter during the day.

249 WEISSENBURGER-PLATZ

Au-Haidhausen ⑤

One of the most beautiful squares in Munich with a cosy atmosphere, located in the French Quarter in Haidhausen. While it's lavishly planted in the summer, in winter the square hosts one of the most romantic and traditional Christmas markets in town. Good for families with children.

250 SANKT-JAKOBSPLATZ

Altstadt-Lehel ①

Our favourite square in Munich. Combining the past and present, where all our city's many themes intersect. Grab a seat on a bench and look around you. If you are travelling with children, they'll like the modern playground between the Jewish Museum and the synagogue.

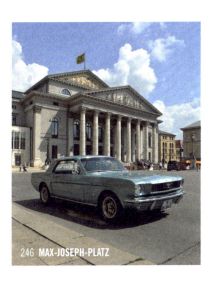

246 MAX-JOSEPH-PLATZ

5 impressive
VIEWS

251 HACKERBRÜCKE

Hackerbrücke
Schwanthaler-
höhe ③

Climbing up the iron Hackerbrücke up to two metres is quite easy because of how it was built. It is a popular haunt for the young crowd for an after-work beer. They look out over the tracks, to the east in the direction of the city centre, with a view of the train station, Frauenkirche and Justizpalast. Or to the west: the direction in which all trains underneath them leave the city, and where the sun sets.

252 CAFÉ ÜBERM MARIENPLATZ

Kaufinger Str. 1-5,
4th Floor
Altstadt-Lehel ①
muenchner-freiheit.de/
cafes/#c-ue-m

This cafe is located on the fourth floor of the Galeria Kaufhof department store and has a beautiful view of the New Town Hall and Frauenkirche and Marienplatz at your feet. In addition, the cakes are of excellent. A good place for a break and for those in the know.

253 OLYMPIABERG

Martin-Luther-
King-Weg
Milbertshofen ④
olympiapark.de/en

Of course, the Olympic Tower has the best views with its viewing platform at 190 metres altitude. However, you'd have to pay to take the lift. A cheaper alternative is climbing Olympiaberg, and you can even see the Alps if the weather is nice.

254 BAVARIA

Theresienhöhe 16
Schwanthaler-
höhe ③
+49 (0)89 290 671

A special view of the city (and the Oktoberfest) can be enjoyed from the Bavaria statue, which is located slightly above Theresienwiese. You can climb right into the statue's head via a spiral staircase. Opening hours vary, during the Oktoberfest they are open until 8 pm.

255 LE BUFFET OBERPOLLINGER

Neuhauser Strasse 18
Altstadt-Lehel ①
+49 (0)89 290 238 97
oberpollinger.de/food-restaurants

This department store, one of the largest in Southern Germany, has a beautiful roof terrace on the fifth floor where you can sit in the sun and enjoy the view over the former stock exchange and the surrounding buildings. They have an affordable international buffet (self-service). There is also a children's play area.

251 VIEW FROM HACKERBRÜCKE

5 ×

MUNICH BY BIKE

---

256 CALL A BIKE
callabike-interaktiv.de

These bikes are available around the clock in over 50 towns and cities. They are very stable and well maintained. You rent them with your mobile phone and you can park and return your bike anywhere you want (within a certain area in the city centre). You can rent by the minute or the day.

257 RADIUS TOURS
Arnulfstrasse 3
Maxvorstadt ③
+49 (0)89 543 487
77 40
radiustours.com

Located right in the city centre in the central train station. They are open seven days a week in summer. Of course, they speak English and you can even rent e-bikes here. The locals mainly know them because of the beer bike tours they organise for tourists, with a line of cyclists ringing their bells all the way through Englischer Garten.

258 PEDALHELDEN
Marsstrasse 11
Maxvorstadt ③
+49 (0)89 516 199 11
pedalhelden.de

Here you can rent almost any special bike you can think of, from professional mountain bikes to all sorts of children's bicycles or cargo bikes. They also rent out children's bike trailers. They also have plenty of fun vehicles such as a 3-person tandem or so-called conference bikes, which carry seven people.

259 SPURWECHSEL

Ohlmüllerstrasse 5
Au-Haidhausen ⑧
+49 (0)89 692 4699
spurwechsel-
muenchen.de

Yes, they also organise beer and bike tours, but they also have plenty of other options, like a football tour or a 19th-century tour. On top of which they rent out bikes so drop in here if you are staying nearby.

260 BIKEBRINGER STEFFEN REHFELDT

+49 (0)173 386 0766
bikebringer.de

Regardless of where you are staying (within Munich), they'll deliver a rental bike to your door and pick it up when you no longer need it. Friendly people, great service. They also rent out child-friendly accessories such as seats, trailers and helmets.

258 PEDALHELDEN

5
ROADS TO FOLLOW

261 AUGUSTENSTRASSE
Maxvorstadt ③

Augustenstrasse is not particularly beautiful in the traditional sense, although it does end in lovely Josephsplatz (visit the farmer's market here every Tuesday). Instead, the street is very popular because of its mix of different shops, cafes, snack bars and restaurants. It's quite lively and leads right into town.

262 TÜRKENSTRASSE
Maxvorstadt ③

Don't miss Türkenstrasse, which you'll probably cross anyway when visiting the Pinakotheken. Walk northwards and you'll discover plenty of shops, lovely cafes, university life and much more. From bustling sections to quieter pockets, Türkenstrasse has it all.

263 LEDERERSTRASSE
Altstadt-Lehel ①

This narrow street in the centre of the old town has lots of historical buildings and takes its name from the leatherworkers and tanners, who used to work here. Here you can experience real Munich, with a captivating mix of listed façades, trendy restaurants and independent shops, loved by locals and tourists alike. And check out '1001 senses', which specialises in unusual and rare types of chocolate.

264 SEDANSTRASSE
Au-Haidhausen ⑤

This road, which is quite typical for the Haidhausen district with its many well-preserved old buildings, is lined with several alternative pubs and cafes as well as unusual shops. It's close to several squares in the area, which makes it a great starting point for exploring this neighbourhood.

265 RUMFORDSTRASSE
Altstadt-Lehel ②

Rumfordstrasse is set back a little from the large nearby squares and offers a lot of variety, including fashion stores, several great furniture stores, two fabulous bookstores and lots of different food options. A stroll along Rumfordstrasse is always fun.

5 local favourites at the
OKTOBERFEST

---

266 OIDE WIESN

Families with children, but also all other visitors, who prefer a slightly less hectic Oktoberfest experience, come here. Yes, they do charge an entrance fee of three euro, but all the rides inside are priced at only one euro. It's all about enjoying traditions from the good old days. Very charming, quite relaxed!

267 STANDKONZERT AN DER BAVARIA

On the second Sunday of Oktoberfest, they organise a traditional concert here at 11 am. The musicians of all the brass bands, that play in the tents, gather below the Bavaria statue where they perform a concert with plenty of Bavarian marches and melodies. Thousands of balloons rise into the sky during the grand finale, when they play the Bavarian anthem.

268 **MITTAGSWIESN IM ZELT**

Join the locals on their lunch break. On working days you can buy some good food here at lower prices. People from the nearby offices meet for a quick break and enjoy some Bavarian specialities at a discount (over mainly non-alcoholic drinks).

269 **SMALLER TENTS**

The smaller tents are often the cosier ones. They are more convivial and you still have the chance to bag a seat when the big tents are long closed due to overcrowding.

270 **TEUFELSRAD**

Even if you do not understand a word, make sure to come here. This archaic spectacle has trilled locals for over 100 years. There is a big disc in the middle, everyone tries to get onto it (they call certain groups of people), then the disc slowly starts to spin and people start falling off. The one, who manages to hang on the longest, wins. Meanwhile, the host makes really mean jokes (in Bavarian) about the participants. Be careful when wearing short trousers as there is a risk of painful blisters.

5

GREEN OASES

to relax

---

271 BOTANISCHER GARTEN

Menzinger Strasse 61
Neuhausen-
Nymphenburg ⑦
+49 (0)89 178 613 16
botmuc.de/en

The Botanic Garden (do not confuse it with the Old Botanic Garden close to the main station!) is a green oasis on the edge of the Nymphenburg Palace Park. Many tourists turn around at the entrance, which is a big mistake, because there's an admission fee . Here you'll find rare botanic species and, above all, a green oasis, a paradise in the city where time seems to have stood still. Careful, the gates really close on time in the evening.

272 KABINETTSGARTEN

Alfons-Goppel-
Strasse
Altstadt-Lehel ①

One of the Residence's courtyards was turned into the garden of the cabinet, an idyllic and quiet place with a water feature, which is a perfect place to seek some peace and quiet. Enter through Marstallplatz. The narrow gate is just opposite the Instituto Cervantes.

271 **BOTANISCHER GARTEN**

273 FINNERL'S GARTENOASE

near Schreberweg 31
Bogenhausen ⑤
+49 (0)89 470 4375

Allotments are a typically German thing. Although they initially were for growing vegetables, today they are a little green heaven for many, with sites scattered all over the city. There are strict rules about what tenants are allowed to do and what they aren't. Watch the hobby gardeners as they work away. The beer garden is open to the public and serves good simple food.

274 BAUMSCHULE BISCHWEILER

Sachsenstrasse 2
Untergiesing ⑧
+49 (0)89 233 604 23

The council gardeners try out plants here for robustness. Over the decades, it has become a real idyll, and it's open to the public. There are different sections like roses, perennials, educational gardens or poisonous plants and a great playground.

275 HOFGARTEN

Hofgartenstrasse 1
Altstadt-Lehel ①

Do you need a break in the city centre? Just come here. Take a stroll like the kings once did. Rest comfortably on one of the numerous benches and sometimes you might even hear music emanating from the pavilion. Diana's temple is the centre of the baroque garden.

5 sights in the
CAPITAL OF SOCCER

---

276 WATCHING A BAYERN TRAINING SESSION
Säbener Strasse 51-57
Giesing ⑧
+49 (0)89 699 310
fcbayern.com/de/
club/saebener-strasse/
besucher-info

It is almost impossible to get tickets for a Bayern match in the Munich stadium. But you can watch the pros while they train. There is not even an admission fee, you get to be quite up close and personal with the players, along with the other fans and you can experience professional football.

277 H'UGO'S
Promenadeplatz 1-3
Altstadt-Lehel ①
+49 (0)89 221 270
hugos-pizza.de/home

It is said that many Bayern players like to eat here. This interesting piece of information is probably one of the reasons why the 'celebrity' quota is relatively high here even if an international audience will have no idea who most of these starlets are.

278 ALLIANZ ARENA
Werner-Heisenberg-
Allee 25
Schwabing ④
allianz-arena.com/en

The football stadium offers various adventure tours, as well as hosting a permanent exhibition on FC Bayern. For die-hard fans.

279 STADION AN DER SCHLEISSHEIMER-STRASSE

Schleissheimer-strasse 82
Maxvorstadt ③
+49 (0)89 529 736
stadionander-schleissheimerstrasse.de

This is not a stadium, but a football-themed pub. Football fans from various Munich clubs meet here to indulge in their passion and watch important matches together. The pub is strictly non-partisan, up to three matches are shown at the same time of German teams but also of many international leagues.

280 FAN ARENA MÜNCHEN

Arnulfstrasse 16-18
Maxvorstadt ③
+49 (0)89 593 115
fanarena-muenchen.de

You'll know at a glance which fans frequent this pub. Everything is red and white, all the walls and the ceiling are decorated with flags and scarves of FC Bayern everywhere. You can admire the many souvenirs and gadgets while you watch a match here.

280 FAN ARENA MÜNCHEN

The 5 most interesting
GUIDED TOURS

281 MVG MÜNCHENTRAM

Max-Weber-Platz
Au-Haidhausen ⑤
mvg.de/services/
freizeittipps/
muenchentram.html

From May to October, Munich's public transport system offers guided city tours in a historic tram. You are driven around the city for one hour and get to see many sights. A tour that is also very popular with locals. The audio information is only in German.

282 STATTREISEN

Nymphenburger
Strasse 149
Neuhausen-
Nymphenburg ⑦
+49 (0)89 544 042 30
stattreisen-muenchen.de

For over 20 years, this company has organised guided city walks, focussing on the classic sights, as well as offering special themed tours. The tours are available in German and in several foreign languages.

283 TOURISMUSAMT MÜNCHEN

+49 (0)89 233 965 00
munich.travel/en-
gb/categories/book/
guided-tours

The city of Munich trains city guides, who undergo extensive examinations before they are allowed to show tourists around the city. Here you are always in good hands, whether you are interested in the classical sights or in tours on other topics.

284 MUNICHWALKTOURS

+49 (0)89 242 317 67

munichwalktours.de/en

They offer the usual tours: historic centre, beer and brewery, food tasting in Viktualienmarkt and the Third Reich.

285 HEYMINGA

+49 (0)89 215 442 05

heyminga-touren.com

These tours in colourfully painted Volkswagen buses, that are already several decades old, are new to the tourist market. The buses whizz through the city for several hours and stop at the sights. Groups are quite small as you can only fit eight people in the bus.

281 MVG MÜNCHENTRAM

5 *magical*
CEMETERIES

286 ALTER NORDFRIEDHOF
Arcisstrasse 45
Maxvorstadt ③

No one has been buried in this cemetery since 1944. As a result, it has become a mix of a cemetery and a park, with a special atmosphere. The tombs are still there, but people come here for picnics or to go jogging. There is a beautiful and very popular playground nearby.

287 ALTER SÜDFRIEDHOF
Thalkirchner Str. 17
Isarvorstadt

Many famous Munich personalities are buried in the South Cemetery, which was originally designed as a plague cemetery. There has not been a funeral here for over 70 years however. Nowadays it's listed as an art and cultural-historical monument and has become a little haven of peace and quiet in the city centre.

287 ALTER SÜDFRIEDHOF

288 NEUER ISRAELITISCHER FRIEDHOF

Garchinger Str. 37
Schwabing ④

Several cemeteries in Munich were designed as forest cemeteries, including the New Israelite Cemetery. Jews consider cemeteries as a symbol of the transience of all being, which is why the tombstones are always maintained. A memorial commemorates the victims of persecution under the National Socialist dictatorship from 1933 to 1945. No visits are possible on Saturdays and on Jewish holidays. You need to cover your head.

289 FRIEDHOF AM PERLACHER FORST

Stadelheimer Str. 24
Obergiesing ⑧

This cemetery, which is located right next to Stadelheim prison, is where some of the numerous victims of National Socialism that were killed in the prison were hastily buried. There are several monuments and honorary shrines in the cemetery today for victims of the Nazi Regime and World War II.

290 FRIEDHOF BOGENHAUSEN

Bogenhauser
Kirchplatz
Bogenhausen ⑤

This little graveyard looks like that of a small village. There are just 208 tombstones here. Only people who lived nearby – or were prominent – are allowed to be buried here. Actors, writers, entrepreneurs and many other prominent figures of contemporary history have found their final resting place here.

BEER
highlights

291 GIESINGER BRÄU

Martin-Luther-
Strasse 2
Untergiesing-
Harlaching ⑧
+49 (0)89 550 621 84
giesinger-braeu.de

This young brewery was founded in 2006 in a backyard. Their aim is to create more variety by producing typical Munich beers as well as other speciality beers. Until recently, this was nearly unheard of in the city. They only use traditional methods. All their beers are made from regional raw materials, are unfiltered and not thermally treated. There is a restaurant and a pub here. Worth a visit.

292 RICHELBRÄU

Richelstrasse 26
Neuhausen-
Nymphenburg ⑦
+49 (0)89 132 584
richelbraeu.de

This microbrewery is a non-commercial, private undertaking. Twice a month, you can take part in a brewing course with a snack, beer tasting and a presentation of the project.

293 HOPFENHÄCKER

Weissenburger
Strasse 16
Au-Haidhausen ⑤
hopfenhaecker.de

A German brewing tradition or an American craft beer? These guys combine the two, creating stunning craft beers with a traditional twist. You can drop in and buy beer directly from the brewery every Friday and Saturday.

294 **SPATEN-FRANZISKANER BRÄU**
Marsstrasse 46-48
Neuhausen-Nymphenburg ⑦
franziskaner-weissbier.de/ext/visitorcenters/en

Now for a different scale of beer production. This brewery has a centuries-long tradition. It is part of one of the world's largest brewery groups, Anheuser-Busch InBev. There is a visitor centre. This is only a bottling plant.

295 **BIER- UND OKTOBERFEST-MUSEUM**
Sterneckerstrasse 2
Altstadt-Lehel ①
bier-und-oktoberfestmuseum.de

You may suspect the worst from a museum that is called the Beer and Oktoberfest Museum but the visit is actually really interesting. The Munich breweries have restored one of the oldest surviving townhouses, the exhibition is interesting and the pub in the museum serves good Bavarian cuisine and beer of course.

295 BIER- UND OKTOBERFESTMUSEUM

5 noteworthy
INSTITUTIONS

296 LITERATURHAUS

Salvatorplatz 1
Altstadt-Lehel ①
+49 (0)89 291 9340
literaturhaus-
muenchen.de

The Literaturhaus might not be ranked the highest of sights, but is one of the most important addresses of literary life in Munich. Here you can enjoy readings, exhibitions change regularly and the cafe is definitely worth a visit, too. Take the lift up to the top floor to admire the stuffed bear that once stood in the family home of Thomas Mann.

297 ESO SUPERNOVA

Karl-Schwarzschild-
Strasse 2
Garching bei
München
supernova.eso.org

Located at ESO Headquarters in Garching bei Munich, the brand-new ESO Supernova Planetarium & Visitor Centre offers an immersive visiting experience that puts the universe we live in in a whole new perspective. Through innovative techniques, and exciting visuals the most abstract topics in astronomy and physics become clear. Be sure to book your tour in advance – many of them are free.

298 AMERIKAHAUS

Karolinenplatz 3
Maxvorstadt ③
+49 (0)89 552 5370
amerikahaus.de

The America House was originally founded by the American military authorities in 1945 as an American Reading Room, a library that was to re-educate and democratise the German people. Today it is run by the Bavarian state and works as an open house for transatlantic exchange and organises a wide and varied range of events. The listed building has recently been renovated and is definitely worth a visit.

299 JÜDISCHES MUSEUM

Sankt-Jakobs-Platz 16
Altstadt-Lehel ①
+49 (0)89 233 960 96
juedisches-museum-muenchen.de

The Jewish Museum Munich opened its doors in 2007. Why it took so incredibly long is an even longer story. Today it's impossible to imagine Munich without it, it has enriched the city with changing exhibitions and is the ideal starting point from which to explore Jewish life.

300 WANNDA

Changing locations
wannda.de

A temporary 'cultural circus' on unused spaces, a kind of city encampment that for a short time turns into a pulsating space, Wannda mostly combines different experiences like yoga, electronic music and art exhibitions. You'll need to check their website and if you're lucky you'll experience something truly different.

5 × remarkable
ARCHITECTURE

---

301 SHARING FRIENDS

Birketweg
Neuhausen-
Nymphenburg ⑦
bauwerk.de/en/object/
friends

Ambitious contemporary architecture has been quite a contentious subject in Munich. In recent years, many new buildings emerged along the railway tracks that lead to the main station. These areas are largely characterised by architectural mediocrity. The residential apartment buildings by the architects Allmann Sattler Wappner, called 'Sharing Friends', are the exception to the rule. Many of the large, square windows transform into bay windows, creating two iconic towers.

302 MESSESTADT RIEM

Trudering-Riem

Over the years, a new neighbourhood was developed on the grounds of the former airport in Riem. They have built an exhibition centre, housing and a large green area, called Riemer Park with a large lake. Take a walk around the neighbourhood to see different ideas about architecture and urban development in practice.

303 BIBLIOTHEK HOCHSCHULE MÜNCHEN

Lothstrasse 13-D
Neuhausen-
Nymphenburg ⑦
andreasmeck.de/p-
ehb-b1.htm

In many cases, the architectural impulses in Munich come from public buildings. Here is a rather unpretentious but nice example. The Central Library of the University of Applied Sciences Munich was extended with a cube-shaped building, which you can access through a bridge on the third floor (you can visit it, it's a public building). The reading room is at the top of the building.

304 BORSTEI

Franz-Marc-Strasse
Moosach ⑦
borstei.de

This ensemble was built between 1924 and 1929 by Bernhard Borst, a contractor and architect. He wanted to combine the beauty of a family house with the practicality of a flat. He believed in relieving women of housework, creating comfort and a pleasant environment. The complex consists of more than 70 contiguous residential buildings with numerous green spaces. Definitely worth a walk.

305 SCHWABINGER TOR

Leopoldstrasse 184
Schwabing ④
schwabinger-tor.de

A small neighbourhood was developed, not far from the Münchner Freiheit, which some believe represents the future of Munich. Modern and predominantly luxurious dwellings in apartment buildings, which are very densely spaced, leaving little room for anything else. The entire area is privately owned and consists mainly of rental apartments. You can only park underground.

5 *exceptional*
ANNUAL EVENTS

306 TANZ DER MARKTFRAUEN
Viktualienmarkt
Altstadt-Lehel ①

On Shrove Tuesday, numerous celebrations take place in the city centre. A local tradition is the dance of the women stallholders of Viktualienmarkt. They wear unusual costumes that refer to their stall. You can see who sells what in the market, whether a baker, butcher or florist. Good to know: it can get rather crowded, show time is at 11 am.

307 AUER DULT
Mariahilfplatz
Au-Haidhausen ⑤
auerdult.de

Dult is a cult. This festival is organised three times a year: in May, July and October. A market, that is all about crockery and rare objects, from house-wares to knife sharpeners, from ceramics to hats, historical postcards, old silver cutlery, records and vintage furniture. There is also plenty of food, fun and entertainment to be had.

308 KOCHERLBALL

**Chinesischer Turm
Schwabing** ③
haberl.de/kocherlball

In the 19th century, domestic workers met every Sunday before mass to dance under the Chinesischer Turm. After a while, this custom was banned, but picked up again in 1989. Ever since then, on one Sunday in July, from the very early morning hours, there is dancing (and drinking) with a live oompah band in the tower. They give short introductions to the traditional dances. Lots of people turn up, often at the end of their night out, many of them in traditional costume and hats.

309 SOMMER-TOLLWOOD

**Olympiapark Süd
Schwabing** ④
tollwood.de

This 3-week festival in June/July is a mixture of a cultural spectacle in a tent city, with alternative ideas and commercial trinkets. Definitely a great way to spend a nice evening in the open air, with many people from Munich and the surrounding rural areas.

310 STARKBIERFEST
AT: LÖWENBRÄUKELLER

**Nymphenburger
Strasse 2
Neuhausen-
Nymphenburg** ⑦
loewenbraeukeller.com

During Lent, they brew strong beer in Bavaria. There are special events with traditional as well as party music. On Friday and Saturday nights at Löwenbräukeller, women can participate in beauty competitions and win a *Dirndl*. Men might want to consider the traditional stone lifting on stage (you need to lift 508 pounds). Caution: this strong beer contains much more alcohol than ordinary lager or ale.

OKTOBERFEST MONUMENT

20 ITEMS RELATED TO MUNICH HISTORY

5

'DARK CHAPTERS'
of history

---

311 MONUMENT TO KURT EISNER

Schmidtstrasse 2
Altstadt-Lehel ①

Kurt Eisner was the leader of the November Revolution in 1918 and also Bavaria's first Prime Minister. In 1919, he was shot here. A memorial plaque was finally put after 70 years and a long, at times turbulent debate. The monument consists of a bronze plaque bearing a relief of the outline of his body and a commemorative inscription.

312 ERINNERUNGSORT OLYMPIA-ATTENTAT

Kolehmainenweg
Milbertshofen ④

This memorial site is dedicated to the twelve victims of the Munich massacre during the 1972 Olympics. The assassins killed eleven Israeli athletes and one German policeman. The video installation loop focusses on the lives of the victims. It is open 24/7 and quite impressive, adding an element of history to your visit of the Munich Olympiapark.

313 PLANE CRASH IN THE CITY CENTRE

Martin-Greif-Strasse/
Bayerstrasse
Schwanthaler-
höhe ⑥

On 17 December 1960, a twin-engine passenger aircraft operated by the U.S. Air Force crashed shortly after take-off, hitting, among others, a crowded tram in the city centre. The plane grazed the steeple of Paulskirche and crashed in the area of Bayerstrasse / Martin-Greif-Strasse (north of Theresienwiese). The full load of fuel set the street ablaze within seconds. In total, 52 people died, including all the passengers and crew and people on the ground. The calamity sparked a debate about a new airport, to be built outside the city boundaries. A commemorative plaque was installed on the pavement at the southwest corner of the crossroads.

314 NSU

Nymphenburger
Strasse 16
Neuhausen-
Nymphenburg ⑦

The terror trial against five individuals who were accused of being involved in the terrorist attacks of the far-right National Socialist Underground (NSU) terror cell started here in 2013. The group carried out two bombings and robbed 15 banks, killing nine migrants and a policeman in the process. To date, nobody understands why the NSU was not stopped earlier. A chapter of German history that is unclosed, as the wounds are still very fresh.

315 OKTOBERFEST BOMBING

Bavariaring 5
Schwanthaler-
höhe Schwanthaler-
höhe ⑥

The bombing on 29 September 1980 is considered the most serious terrorist attack in German post-war history. Thirteen people were killed and 211 injured after the explosion of a device near the main entrance of the Oktoberfest. To this day, the question of whether the single attacker really acted alone has not been solved, not even by the authorities. A new inquiry was launched 35 years after the attack. The monument was inaugurated in 2008.

5

MEMORIALS
relating to the NAZI ERA

316 **EHRENTEMPEL**

Arcisstrasse 12
Maxvorstadt ③

These two structures were erected by the Nazis in 1935 to house the sarcophagi of sixteen party members who had been killed in a failed beer hall putsch in 1923. In 1947, they were destroyed by the U.S. Army as part of denazification. Since then, only the foundation bases remain. In German, we have a saying about letting grass grow over unwanted memories. That is just what happened here, as the ruins were overgrown with rare vegetation and have since become an officially registered biotope.

317 **WUNDEN DER ERINNERUNG**

Corner Schelling-
Ludwigstrasse
Maxvorstadt ③

This art installation from the nineties is part of a European art project, with which the artists wanted to document the scars of World War II. The bullet holes behind the glass seem to have been preserved. The artists wanted to leave the wounds open, to prevent them from healing and ensure that people would not forget. There are three of these 'wound' sites in Munich, and another 12 in Europe.

319 NS-DOKUMENTATIONSZENTRUM

318 KINDERHEIM

Antonienstrasse 7
Schwabing ④

There used to be an orphanage here, where Jewish children lived until their deportation in 1941. The memorial from 2002 was installed in front of the building, because the owners did not agree to a plaque on the actual building.

319 NS-DOKUMENTATIONS ZENTRUM

Max-Mannheimer-
Platz 1
Maxvorstadt ③
ns-dokuzentrum-
muenchen.de

The centre, which is located near the Brown House (the NSDAP headquarters), wants to help people acknowledge, learn and understand the history of this location. Shortly after the war, concerned citizens of Munich clamoured for such a history. It was finally inaugurated in 2015, after a long and tedious decision-making process. 'Why should this still concern me today?', is the question all visitors are asked to think about.

320 DENKSTÄTTE WEISSE ROSE

Geschwister-Scholl-
Platz 1
Maxvorstadt ③
+49 (0)89 218 030 53
weisse-rose-stiftung.de

The history of the White Rose student resistance group is closely linked with Munich. It has often been told and continues to a moving chapter in German history. A group of students and one of their professors campaigned against the Nazi regime. Many of them were arrested and sentenced to death in 1943. Go to the main building of the Ludwig-Maximilians-University to visit the memorial and permanent exhibition.

5 places of
ROYAL HERITAGE

---

321 RESIDENZ
Residenzstrasse 1
Altstadt-Lehel ①

Munich was once the capital of a kingdom and home to the royal family. Their passion for art and architecture shaped the city you are visiting today. Germany's largest castle in a city served as the residential and governmental seat of the rulers for over five centuries. See the splendid surroundings in which the monarchs lived.

322 SCHLOSS NYMPHENBURG
Schloss Nymphenburg 1
Neuhausen-Nymphenburg ⑦

In the old days, this summer residence was situated outside the city boundaries. This is where kings once enjoyed a stroll and lived a life of leisure. To this day, the man who would most likely be king if Bavaria was still a monarchy lives in a side wing of the palace. Munich's residents prefer to spend some time in the adjoining park.

324 **KÖNIGSPLATZ**

323 **SISSI**

Sissi (her real name being Empress Elisabeth of Austria, *née* Elisabeth of Bavaria) is still a very popular figure. She was born in Munich in 1837 and Elisabethstrasse, Elisabethplatz and the Elisabeth market are all named after her. Don't look for the house where she was born, it is no longer there. If you do want to follow in her footsteps, then head to the Hofbräuhaus for a beer. The Empress liked to go there incognito.

324 **KÖNIGSPLATZ**
Maxvorstadt ③

Königsplatz is considered one of the architectural highlights of 'Athens on the Isar', as Munich is sometimes also called. In the 19th century, King Ludwig I had his architects design a series neoclassical buildings and squares, including Königsplatz. From 1933 onwards, it was used by the Nazis, both for public book burnings and for parades. Today the area around Königsplatz is home to Munich's gallery and museum quarter.

325 **ST. MICHAEL CHURCH**
Neuhauser Strasse 6
Altstadt-Lehel ①

This church in the city's car-free zone was built in the 16th century. As well as being a magnificent building, the crypt also contains the tombs of 36 royals. Most of them were buried without their hearts, which were buried separately in Altötting. St. Michael's is the church of the nearby Jesuit monastery, which has earned a lot of respect for the social work the monks do.

5 recent
EVENTS OF INTERNATIONAL INTEREST

326 **OEZ**
Hanauer Strasse 68
Moosach ⑦

When a shooting occurred near the mall Olympia-Einkaufszentrum (OEZ) in 2016, the city ground to a halt for hours and remained in shock for a long time after. One year later, a small memorial was inaugurated, commemorating the victims, and paying tribute to the nearby residents, who helped out and provided shelter to the many people who were unable to get home in the chaos.

327 **SCHWABINGER KRAWALLE**
Leopoldstrasse
Schwabing ④

In June 1962, students clashed with the police in the Schwabing district for four days with some 40.000 rioters taking to the streets in anti-authoritarian riots. What prompted the uprising? More cultural self-determination, youthfulness, a desire for change. Today these events are seen as the harbinger of the 1968 student protest in Germany.

328 STARNBERGER FLÜGELBAHNHOF

Arnulfstrasse 3
Maxvorstadt ③

There were chaotic scenes at this train station in 2015, when tens of thousands of refugees arrived on trains in this station and underwent a first medical exam in this section of the station. Soon the pictures of how the people of Munich welcomed them went viral. Volunteers rushed to the station, distributed food, water, blankets and laid the foundation for a new *Willkommenskultur* (welcome culture) even if German society has been bitterly divided on this issue ever since.

328 STARNBERGER FLÜGELBAHNHOF

329 BEER GARDEN REVOLUTION

Georg-Kalb-Strasse 3
Pullach im Isartal

In 1995, a closing restriction, which was perceived as a threat to the beer garden culture, being the quintessential symbol of the Bavarian soul, inspired 25.000 residents to take to the streets to protest. The court wanted the beer gardens to close at 9 pm after complaints by neighbours about the noise levels.
The Bavarian government soon issued new regulations, exempting beer gardens from closing early in the evening.

330 FORMER GURLITT APARTMENT

Artur-Kutscher-
Platz 1
Schwabing ④

More than 1000 precious works of art were discovered in 2012 in an ordinary apartment in Schwabing, including Franz Marc's *Pferde in Landschaft*. The apartment belonged to a man named Cornelius Gurlitt, who lived like a complete recluse with his paintings. Some of the paintings were suspected of having been looted by the Nazi regime during World War II. While the authorities initially seized the collection, it was returned to Gurlitt in exchange for his cooperation to ascertain the rightful owners of the works.

LENBACHHAUS

50 PLACES
TO ENJOY CULTURE

5

INDEPENDENT ART GALLERIES

---

331 SPERLING
Regerplatz 9
Au-Haidhausen ⑤
+49 (0)89 548 497 47
sperling-munich.com

One wouldn't immediately expect to find a gallery in this part of the city. There was a pharmacy here for over a hundred years, before the building was converted into an exhibition space on several levels. The team around Johannes Sperling, the gallery's founder, represents a small group of younger artists who are on the verge of international breakthrough.

332 GALERIE JO VAN DE LOO
Theresienstrasse 48
Maxvorstadt ③
+49 (0)89 273 741 20
galerie-jovandeloo.com

This gallery, which is located just across the road from Museum Brandhorst, specialises in contemporary photography. Its founder Jo van de Loo, who is a photographer himself, has established an open and friendly atmosphere, representing artists who work in various media.

333 BNKR
Ungererstrasse 158
Schwabing ④
+49 (0)89 689 060 620
bnkr.space

BNKR is located in a converted above-ground Nazi-era bunker and specialises in art and architecture. Every year, they ask a different curator to develop an exhibition and programme, that promotes an interdisciplinary dialogue.

334 NIR ALTMAN GALERIE

Ringseisstrasse 4 Rgb
Isarvorstadt ②
+49 (0)89 388 694 455
niraltman.com

This gallery represents national and international contemporary artists. They work with emerging and mid-career artists, many of whom have already exhibited their work around the world. After establishing the Mika Gallery in Tel Aviv in 2010, the owner Nir Altman opened his new space in Munich in 2016, where he hopes to create a global art space.

335 JÖRG HEITSCH GALERIE MÜNCHEN

Reichenbach-
strasse 14
Altstadt-Lehel ②
+49 (0)89 269 491 10
heitschgalerie.de

Jörg Heitsch opened his gallery in 2006 in Gärtnerplatz. He represents contemporary artists such as Jim Avignon, one of Germany's most beloved artists among others. The gallery's branch at Tegernsee exhibits contemporary sculpture.

332. GALERIE JO VAN DE LOO

5 must-sees in the
ALTE PINAKOTHEK

ALTE PINAKOTHEK
Barer Strasse 27
Maxvorstadt ③
+49 (0)89 238 052 16
pinakothek.de

336 THE GREAT LAST JUDGEMENT
By Peter Paul Rubens

The Alte Pinakothek is one of the world's oldest museums and has the second-largest Rubens collection worldwide. This monumental six-metre-high altarpiece is probably the largest painting Rubens ever painted. The whole room was designed around this masterpiece. Guided tours in several languages are available on Saturdays. On Sundays, the admission price is just one euro.

337 RUBENS AND ISABELLA BRANT IN THE HONEYSUCKLE BOWER
By Peter Paul Rubens

Rubens painted this loving self-portrait, with his wife, shortly after they married. The couple is very fashionably dressed and sit hand in hand, as a sign of their union of love through marriage. They are surrounded by symbols of love, including honeysuckle.

338 THE BATTLE OF ALEXANDER AT ISSUS
By Albrecht Altdorfer

This painting portrays the battle between Alexander the Great and the Persian King Darius III at Issus. Thousands of horse and foot soldiers populate the painting, which has been executed in great detail. The landscape, with the setting sun and the crescent moon, refers to the outcome of the battle (Alexander's victory and the defeat of Darius), marking the historical transition from the Persian to the Greek era.

339 SELF-PORTRAIT AT TWENTY-EIGHT YEARS OLD WEARING A COAT WITH FUR COLLAR
By Albrecht Durer

This self-portrait is one of the most significant paintings in the history of art. It dates from 1500 and is considered iconic because of the frontal pose, which is associated with religious art. At the time, this would have been a contentious painting, because of the monumental Christ-like iconography and the fur collar, which was only worn by the nobility. The collar perhaps was his way of claiming greater social status than was afforded to artists at the time.

340 MADAME DE POMPADOUR
By François Boucher

Madame de Pompadour was the mistress of Louis XV. She looks extremely at ease in this casual portrait by Boucher, as you can see from the way her dress fans out and the way she leans back naturally on the divan. She is surrounded by books and drawings, pointing to her modern lifestyle and the political and intellectual influence she had as an educated and emancipated woman.

5 traces of
DER BLAUE REITER/
THE BLUE RIDER

---

341 LENBACHHAUS
Luisenstrasse 33
Maxvorstadt ③
+49 (0)89 233 320 00
lenbachhaus.de

The Blue Rider movement played an important role in German expressionist art in the early 20th century. The group was influenced by two painters: Moscow-born Wassily Kandinsky (1866-1944) and Munich-born Franz Marc (1880-1916). The comprehensive exhibition in Lenbachhaus tells the movement's story and includes major artworks by related artists.

342 PINAKOTHEK DER MODERNE
Barer Strasse 40
Maxvorstadt ③
pinakothek.de/besuch/
pinakothek-der-
moderne

Various major works by Franz Marc, Wassily Kandinsky, Alexei Jawlensky and August Macke, who founded The Blue Rider are exhibited in the Pinakothek der Moderne.

343 MÜNTER HAUS
Kottmülleralle 6
Murnau am
Staffelsee
+49 (0)88 416 288 80
muenter-stiftung.de

The Münter House in picturesque Murnau am Staffelsee in Upper Bavaria was an important place of inspiration for the new artistic movement. It also became an important meeting place of the avant-garde. Definitely a good place to start if you are planning a trip to the surrounding area.

341 **LENBACHHAUS**

344 SUMMERHOUSE IN THE BACKYARD
Ainmillerstrasse 36
Schwabing ④

Kandinsky recalled the following: "We invented Der Blaue Reiter while sitting at the coffee table, in the gazebo. We both loved blue, Marc the horses, I liked the riders". There used to be a summer house in the rear garden at Ainmillerstrasse, in which Kandinsky and Gabriele Münter lived together without being married. It was considered quite scandalous at the time.

345 ARCO PALAIS
Theatinerstrasse 7
Altstadt-Lehel ①

Heinrich Thannhauser's Moderne Galerie, in the beautiful Arco-Zinnenberg Palace, hosted the first exhibition of the work of Der Blaue Reiter. The response to the exhibition was mixed. Its importance for art history only became clear much later. The gallery closed in 1928. Heinrich Thannhauser died in 1934 on the German-Swiss border, while fleeing the Nazi regime.

The 5 best places to find
STREET ART

346 **CANDIDPLATZ**
   Giesing ⑧

Candidplatz is a bit of an urban mess. It is surrounded by intersections and has a massive concrete flyover. A group of locals arranged to have the columns painted by international street artists, with the support of the city council.

347 **MUCA**
   Hotterstrasse 12
   Altstadt-Lehel ①
   +49 (0)89 215 524 310
   muca.eu

Germany's first urban, street and contemporary art museum. This recent art form is invited to engage in a dialogue with other contemporary arts. MUCA hosts temporary exhibitions as well as several events and has a chic restaurant.

348 **DONNERSBERGER-BRÜCKE**
   Schwanthaler-höhe ⑥

One of Munich's largest concrete structures is this eight-lane bridge, also one of the busiest roads in Europe. Its many concrete pillars are a perfect canvas for street artists. To date, sixty artists were invited to create works in this huge open-air art gallery, which doubles as a car park.

346 **CANDIDPLATZ**

349 **VIEHHOF**

349 VIEHHOF

Tumblinger-
strasse 29
Isarvorstadt ②

The only (!) place in Munich, where street art is legal. Works of art often only remain in place for a few hours, before being covered by another one. The site is managed by Bahnwärter Thiel, a cultural centre. In the long term the graffiti will disappear however, because the city wants to redevelop the site.

350 ISAR BRIDGES

Underneath
Friedensdenkmal
Bogenhausen ⑤

Local and international street artists have left their mark on this pedestrian underpass (on the east side of the river). A truly beautiful location because of the light and a nice place for a stroll along the Isar. If you walk south from here, you'll end up at Ludwigsbrücke, which also features some good street art.

5

INSPIRING MUSEUMS

---

351 VERSICHERUNGS-KAMMER KULTURSTIFTUNG

Maximilianstrasse 53
Altstadt-Lehel ① ⑤
+49 (0)89 216 022 44
versicherungskammer-kulturstiftung. de

This art gallery is owned by the foundation of a major insurance company. The temporary exhibitions are dedicated to various aspects of photography. Check before going, but they always host outstanding exhibitions, focussing on a specific theme or photographer. Admission is free.

352 VILLA STUCK

Prinzregenten-strasse 60
Au-Haidhausen ⑤
+49 (0)89 455 5510
villastuck.de

The original luxurious art nouveau interior of the villa Franz von Stuck designed for himself (built 1897/1898) as an artist's studio and private home, has been preserved. At the rear of the villa, you can visit the artist's garden, with Pompeian sculptures and 19th-century artworks. A *Gesamtkunstwerk*, in which life, architecture, art, music and the theatre were combined, where you can now visit interesting modern exhibitions.

353 KUNSTBAU

Luisenstrasse 33
Maxvorstadt ③
+49 (0)89 233 320 00
lenbachhaus.de/das-
museum/architektur/
kunstbau

An originally vacant space, that was left empty for technical reasons when building the U-Bahn under Königsplatz, was transformed into a simple yet spacious exhibition hall in 1994. The stark rooms are a great space for special exhibitions, with light, sound or large format works. A great place for a different take on art.

354 SAMMLUNG GÖTZ

Oberföhringer
Strasse 103
Bogenhausen ⑤
+49 (0)89 959 396 90
sammlung-goetz.de

The Goetz collection is an extraordinary private collection of contemporary art in a stunning exhibition space (designed by Herzog & de Meuron). Visits to the collection are only possible if you register online beforehand. You will be required to select a date and time. A truly unique experience.

355 BAYERISCHES NATIONALMUSEUM

Prinzregenten-
strasse 3
Altstadt-Lehel ②
+49 (0)89 211 2401
bayerisches-
nationalmuseum.de

The Bavarian National Museum is one of the most important – and still very original – museums of decorative arts in Europe. Even though it was heavily damaged in World War II, you can still follow the original tour through the different exhibition galleries, which was developed 100 years ago. The museum is also famous for its religious crib collection.

5 great venues for
LIVE MUSIC

---

356 BACKSTAGE

Reitknechtstrasse 6
Neuhausen-
Nymphenburg ⑦
+49 (0)89 126 6100
backstage.info

Munich's most alternative club, with several spaces including a large outdoor space. A great venue to see a gig by unknown and established bands, with everything from ska to rock. They also organise various parts for metal, rock, indie and hip-hop addicts. They have a nice secluded beer garden, where they serve food and drinks. You can't pretend to know Munich if you haven't been to Backstage at least once.

357 FEIERWERK

Hansastrasse 39-41
Sendling ⑥
+49 (0)89 724 880
feierwerk.de

This nonprofit institution has been supporting art, music and culture for over thirty years. Their idea is to promote various subcultures so they can develop their own dynamic. The live concerts are incredibly varied. Many bands have played their first gig here, before moving on to larger venues. An open-minded and relaxed place.

358 JAZZBAR VOGLER

Rumfordstrasse 17
Altstadt-Lehel ②
+49 (0)89 294 662
jazzbar-vogler.com

A stylish jazz club, with great ambience, good drinks, and some amazing live music. Real jazz aficionados will feel at home straight away. Do go, even if you're not that into jazz. The charming owner will make every effort to ensure you have an enjoyable evening.

359 MISTER B'S

Herzog-Heinrich-
Strasse 38
Isarvorstadt ②
+49 (0)89 534 901
misterbs.de

Small, sometimes very hot, and always packed. Munich's smallest jazz club hosts local and international jazz musicians. Experience jazz the old-fashioned way, in an intimate setting. The owner will mix your cocktails himself. The place is too tiny to accommodate staff.

360 MILLA

Holzstrasse 28
Isarvorstadt ②
+49 (0)89 189 231 01
milla-club.de

Milla was a happy coincidence of a location that became available and a bunch of people who were interested in opening a live music club. Located in Glockenbachviertel, this club hosts anything from indie concerts to jazz jam sessions. A place for people, who really appreciate music and who are always on the lookout for something new.

5 ways to listen to
WORLD MUSIC

---

361 CIRCULO
**Rosenheimer
Strasse 139
Au-Haidhausen ⑤
+49 (0)89 494 888**
circulo.de

This dance school focusses less on how you execute the steps. Here it's all about the joy of dancing. They host parties, festivals and weekly classes, for fans of salsa cubana, zouk / kizomba and bachata. They walk you through the steps at the beginning of each party.

362 RUPIDOO GLOBAL MUSIC CLUB
Changing locations
rupen.de/termine

This club night is held fairly regularly at Ampere, as well as in other locations. It has become a cross-genre, inter-generational event, that overcomes cultural boundaries. Expect new and often unusual danceable music from around the world including global beats, global pop, oriental, latin, afro, cumbia and balkan style.

363 BUNTE KUH FESTIVAL

Hansastrasse 39-41
Sendling ⑥
bunte-kuh-festival.de

Munich's world music festival, which is held every year in spring, usually in February, offering an upbeat mix of culture, music, dance and parties in a wild fusion of genres from around the world. A place where open-minded people meet to have fun together.

364 KLANGFEST GASTEIG

Rosenheimer Str. 5
Au-Haidhausen ⑤
+49 (0)89 480 980
gasteig.de

Once a year, this festival shakes up things at Gasteigs, Munich's main cultural centre, with more than 30 concerts on four stages, including jazz, rock, classical music and lots of world music. Admission is free. A great opportunity to hear new releases.

365 VOLKSMUSIKTAGE FRAUNHOFER

Fraunhoferstrasse 9
Isarvorstadt ②
+49 (0)89 267 850
*fraunhofertheater.
de/fraunhofer_
volksmusikpreis*

Something different if you're not from Germany. This festival has gathered the best of traditional music, from Bavaria and the Alps, and around the world for many years. If you like folk music, whether traditional or in a groovier, more modern style, then check out the concert programme, which runs for six weeks and starts in January.

5 of the best
ART-HOUSE CINEMAS

366 **CINEMA FILMTHEATER**
Nymphenburger Strasse 31
Neuhausen-Nymphenburg ⑦
+49 (0)89 555 255
cinema-muenchen.de

A place of pilgrimage for film fans in Munich and the place to go if you want to see an English-language film in Munich (most films are dubbed in Germany). They were the first to have a surround system, and screen art-house productions as well as live opera broadcasts. Friday night is sneak preview night.

367 **NEUES MAXIM**
Landshuter Allee 33
Neuhausen-Nymphenburg ⑦
+49 (0)89 890 599 80
neues-maxim.de

One of Munich's oldest cinemas was recently completely refurbished. Many of the films they screen in this neighbourhood cinema are shown in their original version (with German subtitles). Very quaint, a nice crowd.

368 **THEATINER FILMTHEATER**
Theatinerstrasse 32
Altstadt-Lehel ①
+49 (0)89 223 183
theatiner-film.de

This fifties-style cinema is gorgeous. They mainly screen French and European film productions, which are shown in the original version with subtitles.

369 WERKSTATTKINO

Frauenhoferstrasse 9
Isarvorstadt ②
+49 (0)89 260 7250
werkstattkino.de

Definitely the cinema that fits the 'art house' definition to a tee. A place that celebrates cult movies. Don't expect to find any blockbusters here.
 Call ahead to find out what's showing.

370 MUSEUM LICHTSPIELE

Lilienstrasse 2
Au-Haidhausen ⑤
+49 (0)89 482 403
muenchen.
movietown.eu

Everyone in Munich knows the Rocky Horror Picture Show because almost every teenager and many people on their first date came here to see this cult film. It has been shown here twice a week for several decades, a fact that was even deemed Guinness Book of Records-worthy, They also screen blockbusters and art-house movies, many of them in the original version with German subtitles.

370 MUSEUM LICHTSPIELE

5

CLUBS FOR DANCING

371 BOB BEAMAN
Gabelsberger-
strasse 4
Maxvorstadt ③
bobbeamanclub.com

One of Munich's best clubs for hip-hop and house, which became internationally-renowned soon after its opening, for the sound (they have one of the best sound systems in the city) and the revolutionary new light concept. Hip-hop and house for a sophisticated audience.

372 HARRY KLEIN
Sonnenstrasse 8
Altstadt-Lehel ①
+49 (0)89 402 874 00
harrykleinclub.de

A rather small and clearly laid-out venue known for its excellent electro dance music. Fair prices and a more personal club culture. The visuals on the wall, which are just as important as the music, are their trademark.

373 BLITZ
Museumsinsel 1 /
via Ludwigsbrücke
Au-Haidhausen ⑤
+49 (0)89 380 126 561
blitz.club

Their state-of-the-art sound system is perfect for electronic beats. Everyone who dances here loves the amazing vibe and wants to feel it. They have a strict no-photo policy so everyone can enjoy themselves. A club with an interesting creative concept.

374 PARADISO TANZBAR

Rumfordstrasse 2
Isarvorstadt ②
+49 (0)89 263 469
paradiso-tanzbar.de

'Living on my own'... This is where Freddie Mercury shot that infamous video. But other major stars of the seventies and eighties also dropped in. A great place for a happy party, with its long history, the plush red velvet, large mirrors and heavy crystal chandeliers. A popular venue for bachelorette parties, too.

375 S-A-U-N-A

Marsstrasse 22
Maxvorstadt ③
s-a-u-n-a.de

A great place for a party. Here it's all about fun, not posing or looking good. The outdoor area is a great place to cool off as it can get very hot inside (sauna, get it?). You'll need that breath of fresh air once you've managed to make your way through the crowd. Different music genres.

373 **BLITZ**

The 5 best
SEASONAL FESTIVALS

---

376 DOK.FEST
Various locations
dokfest-muenchen.de

One of Europe's largest documentary film festivals. Every year in May, they show the most interesting and relevant international documentaries. DOK.fest is listed in the filmographies of outstanding filmmakers, supports directors from so-called 'low production countries', works on a widespread impact of artistic documentary films and initiates sustainable relationships between established filmmakers and newcomers.

377 THE PINK CHRISTMAS MARKET
Stephansplatz
Isarvorstadt ②
pink-christmas.de

A gay-themed Christmas market, which opens its doors at the end of November. It's rather small – but fun and colourful – and more communicative than any other Christmas market. Lesbians, gays, transgenders, families and neighbours feel equally at home here and look forward to the friendly atmosphere, the rather unusual goods on offer, mulled wine, and the unique evening show performances that take place every day at 7 pm.

378 JAPANFEST

AT: ENGLISCHER GARTEN,
NEAR HAUS DER KUNST
Altstadt-Lehel ①

Every year in July, a Japanese festival is held in Englischer Garten, near the Japanese Teahouse that was built here in the 1970s. The festival is hosted by the Japanese community, and includes dances, martial arts demonstrations, exciting insights into Japanese culture and delicious food. A fascinating atmosphere, and very family-friendly.

379 VESAKH-FEST

AT: WESTPARK
Sendling ⑥
vesakh-muenchen.de

Buddha's birthday is also celebrated in Munich. And in the right place too, in Westpark, with its Asian gardens, in which traditional temples were installed. The Vesakh festival includes religious ceremonies, meditation and delicious food. Exciting!

380 THEATRON

AT: OLYMPIAPARK
Sendling ⑥
theatron.de

At the rear of the Olympic swimming pool, there is an open-air stage with amphitheatre-shaped seating facing the lake. In July, regional and national bands perform here over a period of several weeks. Admission is free, the event is family-friendly (they distribute ear protection for children) and everyone is in an incredibly happy and relaxed mood while the sun sets and the music continues. Don't miss it!

PALÄONTOLOGISCHES MUSEUM

30 THINGS CHILDREN WILL LOVE

5 favourite
PLAYGROUNDS

---

381 SPIELPLATZ OLYMPIAPARK SÜD

Martin-Luther-King-Weg
Milbertshofen ④

This playground is tucked away in the hills on the southern side of the Olympic Park with plenty of play equipment on different levels, including everything from climbing bridges to futuristic elements. This is a great place to recover from a long walk in the park, especially in summer. The cosy Olympiaalm beer garden is just around the corner.

382 SPIELPLATZ AM MILCHHÄUSL

Veterinärstrasse 16
Maxvorstadt ③

The perfect playground for a break in Englischer Garten. There is a water pump, swings and climbing frames. Parents love to relax in the shade of the old trees and the Milchhäusl kiosk next to the playground has a nice selection of food and beverages.

383 SPIELPLATZ AUF DER INSEL

Auf der Insel
Au-Haidhausen ⑤

This playground is located on one of the islands in the river Isar, near the Deutsche Museum. Here you can make your own cascades with a water pump or dig in the sand. In summer, the Kulturstrand opens nearby so everyone in Munich can enjoy a slice of beach life.

384 ABENTEUER SPIELPLATZ NEUHAUSEN

Hanebergstrasse 14
Neuhausen-
Nymphenburg ⑦
+49 (0)89 155 333
asp-neuhausen.de

This adventure playground is a supervised playground, so please check their opening hours before visiting. It was designed and developed by children for children and is a real paradise for children and a green oasis in the heart of the city.

385 WEISSENSEEPARK

Setzbergstrasse
Obergiesing ⑧

There are several playgrounds in Weissenseepark offering something for everyone: small children can play in the water feature, while older children like to go climbing or explore the site. The park also has several fruit trees where you can pick your own.

382 SPIELPLATZ AM MILCHHÄUSL

The 5 best
MUSEUMS
for children

---

386 PALÄONTOLOGISCHES MUSEUM

Richard-Wagner-
Strasse 10
Maxvorstadt ③
+49 (0)89 218 066 30
palmuc.de/bspg

This is a palaeontological museum, and an academic institution, which is why they are only open Monday to Friday. Admission is free. Come and see the skeletons of dinosaurs and prehistoric mammals. The museum is also open on the first Sunday of the month, offering guided tours and a children's quiz.

387 KINDERMUSEUM

Arnulfstrasse 3
Schwanthaler-
höhe ⑥
+49 (0)89 540 464 40
kindermuseum-
muenchen.de

The children's museum hosts changing exhibitions on a specific theme. Children can join in, play along, try out things and conduct experiments. The idea is to find fun answers to complicated questions in a playful way. Not a large museum, so a great option if you are strapped for time.

388 MÜNCHNER STADTMUSEUM – SOUNDLAB

Sankt-Jakobs-Platz 1
Altstadt-Lehel ①
+49 (0)89 233 223 70
muenchner-
stadtmuseum.de/en

The city museum hosts many different exhibitions, some of which are quite suitable for children. Check out its Soundlab.1. The interactive exhibits encourage visitors to experiment with sound and acoustics. Go ahead, touch the objects and make some noise.

389 VERKEHRSZENTRUM

Am Bavariapark 5
Schwanthaler-
höhe ⑥
+49 (0)89 500 806 762
deutsches-museum.de/
en/verkehrszentrum

This branch of the Deutsche Museum teaches you all about city traffic, travel, mobility and technology, past and present. In other words, you can see lots of cars, trucks and trains here, and you can even explore some of them on the inside. Don't miss the demo model railway and the steam locomotive demos!

390 DEUTSCHES JAGD-UND FISCHEREIMUSEUM

Neuhauser Strasse 2
Altstadt-Lehel ①
+49 (0)89 220 522
jagd-fischerei-
museum.de

Children love this museum, because there are so many stuffed animals to see and you may even touch some of them. The museum teaches visitors more about hunting and fishing with hunting rifles and fishing rods on display. Parts of the exhibition have recently been modernised. The building is equally impressive as it used to be a church.

5

WAYS TO GET WET

---

391 COSIMAWELLENBAD
Cosimastrasse 5
Bogenhausen ⑤
+49 (0)89 236 150 50
swm.de/english/m-
baeder/indoor-pools/
cosima-wellenbad.html

Artificial waves! What more do you need to keep children entertained on a rainy day? The waves are switched on for 15 minutes every hour. On sunny days, head to the outdoor pool with a sunbathing area. Generally less busy on weekdays.

392 FLAUCHERINSELN
Flaucherinseln
Sendling ④

Everyone in Munich flocks to the Flaucher along the Isar, whether they have children or not. You can swim and climb rocks and trees on the island. While it tends to get rather crowded in summer, the atmosphere is still quite unique.

393 WASSERSPIELPLATZ
AT: WESTPARK, CLOSE TO:
Heiterwanger Str. 34
Sendling ④

A huge water playground in the middle of a park. There is a small stream, where you can build dams, and some fun climbing equipment and a long slide. Parents love this playground because of the kiosk, where you can hang out on beer benches. Don't forget to bring swimsuits and towels on a hot day.

394 ENTENBACH

AT: ENGLISCHER GARTEN
near Chinesischer Turm
Schwabing ③

There are many streams in the Englischer Garten. The larger canals can be truly dangerous and are not suited for children. The Entenbach is a great place to play and get your feet wet.

395 DANTEBAD

Postillonstrasse 17
Neuhausen-Nymphenburg ⑦
+49 (0)89 236 150 50
swm.de/privatkunden/
m-baeder/schwimmen/
freibaeder/dante-
freibad.html

On hot summer days, the people of Munich love their public outdoor pools. One such pool is Dantebad, where you'll always find some space to spread your blanket on the grass. They have several swimming pools, a water slide, a toddler's playground and a kiosk where you can buy chips.

394 ENTENBACH

5

FUN ACTIVITIES
with children

---

396 AIRHOP

Ingolstädter Str. 172
Milbertshofen ④
+49 (0)89 708 099 07
*airhoppark.de/
muenchen*

The AirHop Park Munich was an instant success when it opened in 2016. Children and adults can let off some steam at this fantastic indoor trampoline park. You can also play games on the trampolines. Book ahead, the standard slot is one hour.

397 DSCHUNGELPALAST

Hansastrasse 41
Sendling ④
+49 (0)89 724 882 40
*feierwerk.de/
einrichtungen-
projekte/
dschungelpalast*

Enjoy a relaxed Sunday breakfast in the cafe of Dschungelpalast with your family. Tuck into a lavish buffet, with live music, children's cinema and crafts. Everyone will go home feeling happy. The venue is a nonprofit cultural centre and serves breakfast every Sunday from early October to late April.

398 KINDERKUNSTHAUS

Römerstrasse 21
Schwabing ④
+49 (0)89 330 357 70
kinderkunsthaus.de

Children between the ages of 2 and 14 years can decide what they are up for in this fun open art workshop. Here they can paint, build, draw on a computer, or create short films. Both the workshop and the media lab offer a nice selection of creative activities. Children under 10 must be supervised by their parents.

399 ICE SKATING

Prinzregenten-
strasse 80
Bogenhausen ⑤
+49 (0)89 236 150 50
swm.de/privatkunden/
m-baeder/eislaufen.
html

In winter, you can go ice skating on this artificial outdoor skating rink to the tune of… well, they play a lot of different genres here. You can rent skates on the premises. If all that skating made you hungry, then you'll be happy to know that the Aquamarin restaurant serves a selection of simple snacks. On really cold days, you can skate on the Nymphen-burger Canal, near Hubertusbrunnen.

400 KULTIKIDS

Grafinger Strasse 6
Au-Haidhausen ⑤
+49 (0)89 628 344 450
kulti-kids.de

This indoor playground is located in the heating plant of a former dumpling factory. Open from Friday till Sunday. Children between the ages of 1,5 and 10 years can enjoy some fun adventures on the huge slides, the climbing wall, trampolines and other play equipment.

400 KULTIKIDS

The 5 best places to
EAT WITH CHILDREN

---

401 CAFÉ REITSCHULE
Königinstrasse 34
Schwabing ④
+49 (0)89 388 876 0
cafe-reitschule.de

The terrace of this restaurant overlooks the ring of Munich's University riding school. Even today, you can see the horses being prepared for a ride in the Englischer Garten. You can watch the lessons in the old riding hall through the windows from some of the tables in the restaurant.

402 VITS
Rumfordstrasse 49
Isarvorstadt ②
+49 (0)89 237 098 21
vitsderkaffee.de

A chic and cosy cafe, also for families. While the adults enjoy exceptionally good cakes and excellent coffee, the kids can play in the well-kept play area.

403 BAMBERGER HAUS
Brunnerstrasse 2
Schwabing ④
+49 (0)89 322 128 210
bambergerhaus.com

Bamberger Haus is a historic building in the heart of Luitpoldpark and home to an Italian and an Austrian restaurant. While the parents enjoy their meal or a rest in the lounge chairs, the children can play in the huge playground with its large fun maze in the park.

404 AMMOS TAVERNA

**Pilgersheimer
Strasse 60
Untergiesing-
Harlaching** ⑧
+49 (0)89 444 887 57
ammos-taverna.de

A family-friendly Greek restaurant with a cosy outdoor area. One of a few places a Munich family would go for a relaxed meal.

405 GASTSTÄTTE ZUNFTHAUS

**Thalkirchner Str. 76
Isarvorstadt** ②
+49 (0)89 538 865 30
zunfthaus-muenchen.de

A nice, relaxed tavern, where you can enjoy a good homecooked meal away from the hustle and bustle of the neighbourhood. The interior is welcoming in a rustic way, and you can dine out in the yard on summer days. Children love the *Kaiserschmarrrn* (the Emperor's Mess), a shredded fluffy sugar pancake with raisins and apple sauce.

402 **VITS**

5

CULTURAL TIPS

children will love

406 INTERNATIONALE JUGENDBIBLIOTHEK
AT: SCHLOSS BLUTENBURG
Neuhausen-Nymphenburg ⑦
+49 (0)89 891 211 0
ijb.de

Can you think of anything better than visiting an old castle? How about a romantic castle, which has the world's largest library for international children's and youth literature? The collection includes books in many different languages, and you can see exhibitions and much more. There is also a nice restaurant in the castle.

407 BMW FAMILIENSONNTAGE
AT: BMW WELT
Am Olympiapark 1 Milbertshofen ④
+49 (0)89 125 016 001
bmw-welt.com/de/ experience

BMW Welt is a major attraction in Munich. Some useful hints for your visit: if you book well in advance, kids can take a one-hour 'researcher workshop' at the Junior Campus Laboratory, where they conduct experiments under supervision with a quiz at the end. Once a month, they have a 'Family Sunday' with special guided tours.

408 MÜNCHNER PHILHARMONIKER

Rosenheimer Str. 5
Au-Haidhausen ⑤
+49 (0)89 480 985 090
spielfeld-klassik.de

The Münchner Philharmoniker – a world-class orchestra – has a colourful and interesting family-friendly programme, called 'Spielfeld Klassik'. You can attend the conductor's rehearsals with the orchestra for example, where English is spoken or buy tickets for the children's concerts in the family programme. There is always something going on. Please note, the website is available in German only.

409 BAYERISCHE VOLKSSTERNWARTE MÜNCHEN

Rosenheimer
Strasse 145-H
Au-Haidhausen ⑤
+49 (0)89 406 239
sternwarte-
muenchen.de

Munich's public observatory was founded over 60 years ago. Thanks to donations and the helping hands of many volunteers, this has become a little astronomer's paradise. There is a small planetarium, telescopes and much more. English tours are only offered in the evening, so better suited for children aged 12 years and over.

410 BAYERISCHE STAATSOPER

Max-Joseph-Platz 2
Altstadt-Lehel ①
+49 (0)89 218 501
staatsoper.de/en/
campus/children-
young-people

Explore the exciting world of opera, ballet and concerts. Munich's famous opera has a lot to offer for families and children, including young adults as well as younger children. Check out their family performances: children under 18 pay only 10 euro for any seat in the house. What's more, they also organise special workshops and introductions to the performances (in German) for children.

EDEN HOTEL WOLFF

20 PLACES TO SLEEP

5
BOUTIQUE
hotels

411 BAVARIA BOUTIQUE HOTEL
Gollierstrasse 9
Schwanthaler-
höhe ⑥
+49 (0)89 508 0790
hotel-bavaria.com

Their website says: 'A hotel to put you in a good mood'. This lovely hotel is ideal for a short break or a shopping trip. Set in the trendy Westend district, it is a good base to get to the centre of Munich or visit the Oktoberfest.

412 HOTEL IM HOF
Schellingstrasse 127
Maxvorstadt ③
+49 (0)89 700 746 060
hotel-im-hof.de

If you are planning a cultural city trip, then do stay at this charming hotel in the museum quarter, which opened in 2016. It's within easy walking distance of the city's famous art museums, the Pinakotheken, and many art galleries. You can also enjoy culinary delights from around world in the many nearby restaurants, bistros, cafes and typical student bars.

413 CORTIINA HOTEL

Ledererstrasse 8
Altstadt-Lehel ①
+49 (0)89 242 2490
cortiina.com

A hidden secret among Munich's boutique hotels in the heart of the city. The designers selected natural materials such as bog oak and Jura natural stone to create a timeless ambience, which is why locals and tourists alike flock to the Cortiina for afternoon tea, a restaurant dinner or a late-night drink at the bar.

414 HOTEL OLYMPIC

Hans-Sachs-Strasse 4
Isarvorstadt ②
+49 (0)89 231 890
hotel-olympic.de

This hotel offers an interesting blend of elegant and old-fashioned styles. The Olympic is located between Gärtnerplatz and Sendlinger Tor, in the hip district of Glockenbachviertel, which is considered of the most beautiful areas of Munich. While there are plenty of clubs and bars nearby, you'll get a good night's sleep as most of the rooms face the quiet backyard. Famous sites such as Viktualienmarkt and Deutsches Museum are just a short walk from the hotel.

415 BOLD HOTEL

Lindwurmstr. 70-A
Sendling ⑥
+49 (0)89 20001592244
bold-hotels.com

Urban style, nice design and some of the rooms even come with a kitchenette, a balcony or a roof terrace. The furniture in this stylish hotel was designed by Hay and Bloomingville. A great place for design lovers and a good starting point to explore the old district of Sendling. Very good value for money and plenty of rooms.

5

H I P

hotels

416 THE FLUSHING MEADOWS

Fraunhoferstrasse 32
Isarvorstadt ②
+49 (0)89 552 791 70
*flushingmeadows
hotel.com*

Hard to find, although it is located on a very busy corner. While this hotel, which is located on the two top floors of an industrial building, may look non-descript, you'll be blown away when you step inside and see the eleven individual loft studios. The designs are the result of collabs with a musician, a pro surfer, a musician and a DJ, a film director… There are five penthouse studios on the top floor, where you'll also find the public bar.

417 25HOURS HOTEL THE ROYAL BAVARIAN

Bahnhofplatz 1
Altstadt-Lehel ①
+49 (0)89 904 001 255
25hours-hotels.com

This hotel, which is located in the magnificent neo-renaissance building of a former post office, is conveniently close to the city's central station. Munich's first 25hours designer hotel has 165 rooms in five categories. The interior is an interesting take on Bavaria's royal past. Good to know: the hotel offers rental bikes for free. And they know good food as you'll find out when you eat at Neni, the hotel's restaurant.

418 COCOON

Adolf-Kolping-
Strasse 11
Altstadt-Lehel ①
+49 (0)89 599 939 02
cocoon-hotels.de

Stay at one of the three Cocoon hotels if you're into funky seventies retro design. The Eero Aarnio Ball Chairs are real eye-catchers. All three hotels combine a retro ambience with modern amenities, a central location and affordable prices.

419 WERK4

Berg am Laim
adinahotels.com/
wombats-hostels.com

The former potato factory district is currently being redeveloped into a new, modern and lively quarter, called WERK4. Eye-catcher of the district is the old potato silo which is being converted and integrated into an impressive building that will be raised to a final height of 86 metres. The elegant Adina Apartment Hotel will occupy its upper floors, while a lively Wombat's Hostel with 500 beds will open on the lower floors in 2020.

417 **25HOURS HOTEL THE ROYAL BAVARIAN**

420 ROOMERS

Landsberger-
strasse 68
Schwanthaler-
höhe ⑥
+49 (0)89 452 2020
roomers-munich.com

As per their own description, Roomers is 'Electric. Hedonistic. Sexy. Sensual. Luxurious. Glamorous'. More importantly, they have 281 rooms and suites and a Japanese-inspired restaurant, called IZAKAYA. Combining modern luxury with an urban lifestyle. This is also a fun hotel if you love the work of the fine art photographer David LaChapelle.

422 **LUX**

5 ×

GOOD VALUE FOR MONEY

421 RUBY LILLY HOTEL & BAR

Dachauer Strasse 37
Maxvorstadt ③
+49 (0)89 954 570 820
ruby-hotels.com

A leading travel magazine, GEO Saison, recently published its list of Europe's most beautiful hotels, putting the Ruby Lilly in first place in the category 'Hotels under € 100'. The elegant yet welcoming lean and luxurious design is a hit with urban travellers. The cool kids also like to hang out at the Lilly bar, with its 1970s aesthetic, which pays tribute to the Glitterati lifestyle of Munich's TV and film actors.

422 LUX, BAR HOTEL RESTAURANT

Ledererstrasse 13
Altstadt-Lehel ①
+49 (0)89 452 073 00
hotel-lux-muenchen.de

This small and trendy hotel is located in the heart of the old town. A tastefully decorated place with modern rooms at affordable prices. No elevator, you can only get to your room via the beautiful antique spiral staircase. The downstairs bar is very popular with the locals and serves unbelievably creative cocktails.

423 HOTEL MARIANDL

Goethestrasse 51
Isarvorstadt ②
+49 (0)89 552 9100
mariandl.com

Hotel Mariandl is very popular with visitors of the Oktoberfest, as it's very close to the Theresienwiese and reasonably priced. Staying here is like stepping into a time machine. The house was built over 100 years ago and has retained much of its flair, as well as the furniture, with plenty of antiques, old parquet floors, lots of marble, stucco ceilings and crystal chandeliers. No TV, no elevator. Located above the Café am Beethovenplatz.

424 HOTEL AM VIKTUALIENMARKT

Utzschneider-
strasse 14
Altstadt-Lehel ① ②
+49 (0)89 231 1090
hotel-am-
viktualienmarkt.de

This tiny hotel with 26 rooms is just a two-minute stroll from Viktualienmarkt and Gärtnerplatz. The room rates are good value and breakfast is included. And some guests will be happy to know that the new Birkenstock store is just around the corner (Reichenbachstrasse 8).

425 CREATIF HOTEL ELEPHANT

Lämmerstrasse 6
Ludwigsvorstadt ①
+49 (0)89 555 785
creatif-hotel-elephant.de

Combining modern amenities with creative design, this hotel is very close to the city's central station, making it a good starting point for a city tour. Good value for money.

5 hotels
WITH A GOOD STORY

426 DEUTSCHE EICHE

Reichenbach-
strasse 13
Isarvorstadt ②
+49 (0)89 231 1660
deutsche-eiche.com

From around the 1950s onwards, this hotel became a meeting place for artists, hedonists and homosexuals who were still prosecuted back then. Over the years, it became home to a lively scene with famous guests including Rainer Werner Fassbinder and Freddy Mercury. Still a beacon of the gay scene. Their huge men's sauna, on four floors, is open to the public.

427 EDEN HOTEL WOLFF

Arnulfstrasse 4
Altstadt-Lehel ①
+49 (0)89 551 150
eden-hotel-wolff.de

Les Clefs d'Or is the international club of the lobby concierges. You can recognise them by the crossed keys on their lapel. Some of the club's members work in this hotel, which combines a stylish ambience with 130 years of history. The hotel is situated opposite the Haupt-bahnhof. The rooms are decorated in a tasteful Alpine style. Many guests return time and again.

427 **EDEN HOTEL WOLFF**

429 **BAYERISCHER HOF**

428 HOTEL OPERA

Sankt-Anna-Str. 10
Altstadt-Lehel ⓘ
+49 (0)89 210 4940
hotel-opera.de

A beautiful city palace, between Maximilianstrasse and Englischer Garten. Each of the 25 rooms and suites is decorated in its own charming style. The pretty art nouveau façade conceals a beautiful renaissance-style courtyard, which is open for breakfast for external guests. The famous Eisbach River, which is a popular river surfing spot in the English Garden, runs underneath the building.

429 BAYERISCHER HOF

Promenadeplatz 2-6
Altstadt-Lehel ⓘ
+49 (0)89 212 0900
bayerischerhof.de

If you like to sleep where the rich and famous have slept, then this five-star hotel is just the place for you. Built in 1841, it has welcomed Napoleon, Beyoncé, Franz Kafka, Karl Lagerfeld, Grace Kelly and Michael Jackson among others. There is an unofficial memorial opposite the hotel, where fans have been leaving flowers ever since his death.

430 SPLENDID DOLLMANN

Thierschstrasse 49
Altstadt-Lehel ⓘ
+49 (0)89 238 080
splendid-dollmann.de

This hotel, which is situated in an elegant 19th-century townhouse in the heart of Lehel, is especially lovely, with its antique furniture and many beautiful details. But the garden is its real selling point. The writer Erich Kästner lived here after the end of World War II, in a room on the first floor. In those days, it was still a rather unassuming guesthouse. His room became a meeting place for the new cultural scene in the city.

THE WILD ISAR AND ITS TRADITIONAL RAFTS

35 WEEKEND ACTIVITIES

The 5 best weekend
WALKS

---

431 WALK ALONG THE RIVER ISAR
FROM THE ZOO TO REFRESHMENTS IN GROSSHESSELOHE
approx. two hours

This is where the quieter part of the Isar begins. You are gradually leaving the city. Here and there the river is allowed to find its own way so you'll see small bays and gravel islands. Stay on the west side of the river and walk south until you see Grosshesseloher Brücke high up above. The Waldwirtschaft (they play live jazz) beer garden and the little Isarfräulein cafe are a short walk away, up a steep path. To get back to the city, you can take the S-Bahn from Grosshesselohe Isartalbahnhof, which is a 10-minute walk away.

432 FOLLOW THE RIVER WÜRM TO BLUTENBURG CASTLE
approx. 30 min.

The River Isar runs through Munich as well as the smaller Würm River. From Pasing (S-Bahn station), you can take a nice walk along its banks. From Kaflerstrasse (after number 15) turn north onto Hermann-Hesse-Weg. Then follow the water, until you reach the picturesque Blutenburg Castle.

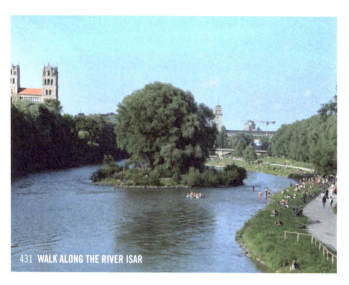

431 WALK ALONG THE RIVER ISAR

434 SANKT EMMERAMSMÜHLE

433 EXPLORE THE FOREST FORSTENRIEDER PARK

approx. 1 hour

Take the metro to Fürstenried West and walk up Maxhofstrasse, which leads right into the huge forest owned by the Bavarian state. You might spot wild boar here or deer as well as old trees and lovely flowers. Take the second path (named Link geräumt) to the left, which leads to a small playground.

434 NORTHERN PART OF ENGLISCHER GARTEN TO SANKT EMMERAMSMÜHLE

approx. 1,5 hours

A walk through one of the world's largest city parks. The northern part of Englischer Garten is much quieter, larger and somewhat wilder than the southern section. Start at Münchner Freiheit, walk to Kleinhesseloher See and take the little bridge over the ring road, then head north. Cross the Isar at the wooden bridge and follow the signs to Emmeramsmühle. A lovely beer garden awaits you here. Return by tram, which stops nearby.

435 THE WILD ISAR AND ITS TRADITIONAL RAFTS

walking time approx. 3 hours including transport

Take the S-Bahn 7 to Wolfratshausen (40 min.). From there, walk north, cross the River Loisach on Weidacher Hauptstrasse. Turn north again immediately. Now you can follow a beautiful path next to the river, until it merges with the River Isar. This stream eventually leads you to Munich. If you're brave – and have booked well in advance, you can take a raft back into town, which takes about 6 hours.

5 visits to the surrounding
LAKES

436 AMMERSEE

The lakes around Munich are especially charming and are all very easy to reach by public transport or by car. The Ammersee's shoreline is almost completely accessible. You can take lovely walks, find a spot to swim, or go on a boat trip. There are nostalgic beaches where you can bathe (Riederau and Herrsching). A rather quiet area is the park of Künstlerhaus Gasteiger (Holzhausen).

437 FELDMOCHINGER SEE

There are several lakes in Munich, in which you can swim. People flock here on sunny days. Barbecues are allowed on the south shore, families prefer the eastern shore because of the playground. Easy to get to by public transport.

438 WALCHENSEE

The Walchensee has a forested shore, the water looks a stunning turquoise. As the winds can be strong here, it's a beautiful surf and kite area. You can relax in the garden of Café Bucherer in the village of Walchensee, where they serve the best cakes ever, or take the cable car to the top of Herzogstand mountain.

438 WALCHENSEE

439 CHIEMSEE

The Chiemsee is Bavaria's largest lake and has some stunning Alpine scenery as a backdrop. It is famous for its royal castle on Herreninsel Island and the Benedictine monastery on nearby Fraueninsel Island. The Christmas market there with its festive lighting resembles a romantic winter fairy tale. In summer, you can take the train to Prien and the steam tram (from 1887!) to the harbour. Buy discounted tickets at the train station.

440 STARNBERGER SEE

It takes about half an hour to get to Lake Starnberg. You can take the S-Bahn to get to several of the beautiful bathing spots. Get off at Possenhofen. 'Paradise' is just a short walk away. The park is part of the grounds of the former Sissi castle. Lots of beaches, playgrounds and a lovely atmosphere. Admission is free.

5

SMALL TOWNS NEAR MUNICH *worth a visit*

441 PULLACH

You easily get to Pullach by S-Bahn. It's close to the Isar valley, so head to Gasthof Rabenwirt or Treibhaus for a spectacular view. The town centre in front of these two restaurants is charming. Peek into the old church and have an ice cream on the square. Pullach is also famous because the headquarters of the German secret service were based here for several decades.

442 MURNAU

A picturesque small town without all the Bavarian kitsch. You can enjoy the mountain views – and especially the Zugspitze – from the pedestrian zone, with its tiny picturesque houses. Gelateria Gabrielli (Untermarkt 9) sells good ice cream. If you plan to stay overnight, check out Gästehaus am Schloss, a Bavarian B&B. See mountains, nearby Staffelsee Lake, and Schwaiganger, a state-owned stud farm. Don't forget to check the list for traces of The Blue Rider.

443 DACHAU

See all of Dachau by visiting the concentration camp memorial and the historic city centre. You can enjoy expansive views of Munich from the terrace of the town hall and from the courtyard garden of Dachau Castle. Munich has influenced the city's fate throughout much of Dachau's history.

444 SCHLEISSHEIM

Visit Schloss Schleissheim. It's just a 20-minute journey by car or public transport, but it feels like travelling back in time. The palace is very quiet and you might even be all by yourself in the avenues of the former royal garden. Enjoy the castle and its grounds and taste the wonderful cakes in either Schlosscafé or Café zum Schloss.

445 FREISING

Throughout the centuries, Freising has been Bavaria's cultural and spiritual epicentre, employing some of the best contemporary builders and artists. The town has a charming mix of old and new and feels very laidback. It is one of the oldest cities in the region and its cathedral's history dates back to 715 AD.

5

SPA VISITS

---

446 SO SPA (SOFITEL)

Bayerstrasse 12
Ludwigsvorstadt ②
+49 (0)89 599 480
*sofitel-munich.com/de/
so-spa/*

A spiral-shaped pool, steam bath, sauna, relaxation rooms with beautiful tiles, as well as a nice range of massages and beauty treatments. The spa of Sofitel Munich Bayerpost fulfils all your wishes if you are looking to unwind. And it's also open to external visitors (by appointment).

447 SAUNA IM WESTBAD

Weinbergerstrasse 11
Isarvorstadt
+49 (0)89 236 150 50
swm.de

Relax in the whirlpool, unwind in the steam cabin, or enjoy the two sauna areas under the large glass cupola of this public family pool. There is also an open-air courtyard with a plunge pool. Sauna and swimming are included in the entrance fee.

448 MÜLLERSCHES VOLKSBAD

Rosenheimer
TheStrasse 1
Au-Haidhausen ⑤
+49 (0)89 236 150 50
*swm.de/english/m-
baeder/indoor-pools/
volksbad.html*

The Müllersches Volksbad's magnificent art nouveau design is simply stunning. The baths opened in 1901 and almost all the historic details have been preserved. The Roman steam bath is the highlight of the sauna facilities. Your body warms up slowly in rooms heated to different temperatures. There is also a Finnish sauna.

449 EMOTION SPA

Bayerstrasse 41
Ludwigsvorstadt ②
+49 (0)89 242 225 50
muenchen.
emotionspa.de

This spa is part of the Méridien hotel. Enjoy the sauna or a massage. You'll feel relaxed and refreshed when you step back out onto busy Bayerstrasse. Day tickets for external guests available. You can rent the entire spa for one night, for just you and your partner.

450 FACE & BODY DAY SPA

Romanstrasse 39
Neuhausen-
Nymphenburg ⑦
+49 (0)89 171 802
dayspa.
faceandbody.de

A place with bright, friendly treatment rooms, including a zen garden, where you can relax and unwind. They have been voted one of Europe's best day spas several times already. Take your pick from an extensive range of treatments.

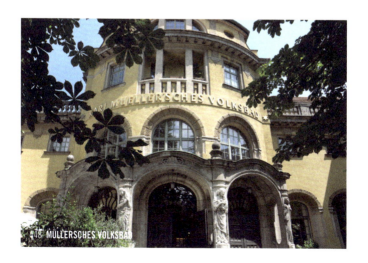

448 MÜLLERSCHES VOLKSBAD

5
SPORTS AND FITNESS
activities

---

451 FIT IM PARK

muenchen.de/freizeit/
sport/gymnastik-im-
park.html

In summertime, the council of Munich offers free training in several public parks. Everyone can get fit for free. Just bring a towel or mat. In addition to traditional fitness, they also offer pilates and yoga.

452 BEACHARENA

Föhringer Ring 5
Schwabing ④
+49 (0)89 322 101 00
beacharena.com

Play (beach) volleyball, beach soccer or tennis. Spend some time with your feet in the sand, in the sun and with other sports enthusiasts, with sun loungers and palm trees. They also serve food here. On most weekends, you can drop in as a team or alone. You'll find the right teammates on every level at their 'Come Together'. Note, they are closed during winter.

453 LEDERHOSEN-TRAINING

AT: ENGLISCHER GARTEN

Schönfeldwiese near
Japanischen Teehaus
Altstadt-Lehel ①
lederhosentraining.
com

Lederhosentraining is a functional training without equipment, and is open to all ages, all sexes, and every fitness level. Every Monday at 7 pm, from April to September, up to 1000 people meet for Munich's largest regular outdoor training. And no, you do not have to wear *Lederhosen*.

454 AMIENA'S WERKSTATT

Müllerstrasse 33,
Hinterhaus
Isarvorstadt ②

Yoga, pilates, barre workout… A lovely studio, with good supervision. No prior registration required.

455 OLYMPIA SCHWIMMHALLE

Coubertinplatz
Schwabing ④
+49 (0)89 236 150 50
swm.de/privatkunden/
m-baeder/schwimmen

Swim your laps, in the pool where all the swimming and diving competitions of the 1972 Summer Olympics were held. The pool is 50 metres long. They also have a sauna area (pay extra), a diving platform and much more. Still an impressive site after all these years.

5 *great*

MOUNTAIN EXPERIENCES

A NOTE FOR ALL HIKING TRIPS: GET ADDITIONAL INFORMATION AND PROPER EQUIPMENT TO AVOID PUTTING YOUR HEALTH AT RISK.

456 ASCHAU KAMPENWAND

The Kampenwand cable car takes you comfortably to almost 1500 m altitude, into the mountains, where you can enjoy imposing rock formations and magnificent views. Once at the top, you'll have a fantastic view of the mountain range. Travel by train to Aschau am Chiemgau, then by bus to the cable car.

457 NATIONALPARK-ZENTRUM – HAUS DER BERGE

Hanielstrasse 7
Berchtesgaden
+49 (0)86 529 790 600
haus-der-berge.
bayern.de

'Experiencing nature with all your senses' is the motto of this 'house of the mountains', which is part of the Berchtesgadener National Park. It combines an information and education centre with an adventure area for nature lovers. There is a lot to discover, including walks, water playgrounds and a herb and vegetable garden.

458 HÖRNLE UNTERAMMERGAU

Each of the three Hörnle peaks rises approx. 1500 m above sea level. You'll have to ascend about 600 metres in altitude from Unterammergau (park at the hiking car park near the church of Kappl). In addition to seeing three peaks in one tour, you'll be rewarded with a fantastic view of the Bavarian mountains and the surrounding peaks. Stop at Hörnle Hütte, where they serve good regional cooking.

459 FROM SCHLIERSEE TO TEGERNSEE

Take the train to Schliersee, a village on the lake with the same name. From there, hike up to Kreuzbergalm for a wonderful view of the lake. Continue in the direction of Gindelalmschneid and Gindelalm, at the same altitude all the way to Neureuth. From here, walk downhill, following the trail to Lieberhof and Tegernsee, another lake, where you can take the train back to Munich. You could leave one hour later and visit the famous local brewery.

460 PARTNACHKLAMM – GARMISCH PARTENKIRCHEN

The Partnach River has cut about 80 metres into the rocks. The walk through this gorge is particularly impressive. Follow the trail (entrance fee ca. 5 euro) through tunnels and past magnificent cliffs to wild water canyons. Very impressive, especially in winter. If it's cold enough, you'll see huge curtain-shaped icicles hanging from the walls. With a little luck, you can also watch ice climbers. Bring warm clothes, even in summer, and a rain jacket, because of the water dripping from above.

5 *fascinating*
ARCHITECTURAL TREKS

461 GEBÄUDE 0505

Luisenstrasse 55
Maxvorstadt ①

Building number 0505 of the Technische Universität was built in 1963 by Franz Hart, who designed several major buildings in the city. Over the years, it became rather rundown. The architects Hild and K developed a concept that rendered the structure of the building – reinforced concrete – visible. They dismantled panels and other interior finishes where possible. Then, they built a new building envelope from the outside. Walk around the building and sneak onto the adjoining campus.

462 WERKSVIERTEL MITTE

Atelierstrasse 4
Au-Haidhausen ⑤
werksviertel-mitte.de

They used to produce potato dumplings here. Then it became a popular nightlife spot. Now they are developing a whole new city district here, which will also include some art and cultural spots. The charm of the existing industrial architecture contrasts nicely with the contemporary new buildings.

463 TRAM 23

**Münchner Freiheit
Schwabing** ④

Tram number 23 has become the perfect way to explore several urban development projects. The route runs through four new neighbourhoods, that were built or changed dramatically in recent years. The ride takes just nine minutes from Münchner Freiheit. It includes the skyscrapers at 'Münchner Tor' and alternative building projects at Domagkpark.

464 PASINGER VILLENKOLONIEN

**August-Exter-Strasse
Pasing** ⑦

Munich's development has often been influenced by investors, who planned entire neighbourhoods in one go. More than 100 years ago, the villa colony of Pasing was created, which is now listed in its entirety as a historic monument. The district has many different architectural styles and lots of trees. A good starting point is August-Exter-Strasse.

465 ARCHITEKTOUREN

**Bayerische
Architektenkammer
+49 (0)89 139 880 0
*byak.de/planen-
und-bauen/
architektur-baukultur/
architektouren.html***

A unique opportunity for anyone interested in architecture. Visit newly finished projects in architecture, landscapes, interior design and urban planning in Munich and Bavaria in June. Architects and their clients provide information about their projects on-site and inform interested visitors.

SOPHIE SCHOLL
1921   1943

35 RANDOM FACTS AND URBAN DETAILS

5

FILMS
about Munich

---

466 KEEP SURFING
2009

In addition to some hair-raising shots of the Eisbach surfers, this film portrays the unusual lives of its protagonists. *Keep Surfing* shows that there is much more to Munich than affluent beer drinkers and pretzel lovers, delving deeper into the city's anarchist heart, and discovering an adventurous and bohemian bunch of river surfers.

467 SOPHIE SCHOLL – DIE LETZTEN TAGE
2005

The last days in the life of Sophie Scholl. A fascinating historical drama. The film won a Silver Bear for best director and best actress (Julia Jentsch) at the 2005 Berlinale and was also nominated for an Oscar.

468 ANGST ESSEN SEELE AUF
1974

One of the more famous films by Rainer Werner Fassbinder. This film tells the story about the relationship between the German window cleaner Emmi and the Moroccan migrant worker Ali. A sensitive portrayal of the disdain for minorities and the mechanisms of social oppression in Western Germany. Filmed in Munich.

469 VISIONS OF EIGHT
1973

Miloš Forman, Yuri Ozerov, Mai Zetterling, Arthur Penn, Michael Pfleghar, Kon Ichikawa, Claude Lelouch and John Schlesinger were asked to focus on one aspect of the Olympic Games in 1972, that seemed important to them. Each director contributed a 15-minute segment, capturing the atmosphere at the Games.

470 MUNICH
2005

This film by Spielberg, which is based on the true story of the Israeli retaliation for the Munich massacre at the 1972 Olympics, mixes facts with fiction. The outcome is an exciting political thriller, which was criticised for its 'moral ambiguity'.

5

BOOKS *in and on Munich*

**471 THE BOOK THIEF
(DIE BÜCHERDIEBIN)**
By Markus Zusak

Set in the fictional village of Molching near Munich before and during the Second World War, brave Liesel learns to read. She escapes the cruel reality of World War II through the power of language and the written word.

472 GLADIUS DEI
By Thomas Mann

This novella, with its famous opening quote ("Munich shone") takes place on a radiant June day in Munich in the late art nouveau era. Thomas Mann ironically attacks the sterile art scene of his time in general, and the thriving Munich Renaissance cult in particular.

**473 SUCCESS
(ERFOLG)**
By Lion
Feuchtwanger

A portrait of Bavaria after World War I. Many of the characters are inspired by real people. Feuchtwanger tells the fictive story of an art historian and museum director, who is quite unpopular because he buys modern and controversial works of art and exhibits them in his state museum.

474 PERFUME (DAS PARFUM)
By Patrick Süskind

An international sensation and one of the most famous German-language novels of the entire 20th century. Interestingly enough, almost nobody knows the author, who lives (mainly) in Munich. Süskind is never seen in public, he refuses awards and does not give any interviews. He did not even attend the premiere of the film adaptation of his novel. So you never know, he might be the man sitting next to you in a cafe when you're in Munich.

475 LOTTIE AND LISA (DAS DOPPELTE LOTTCHEN)
By Erich Kästner

This children's book was written by Erich Kästner in Munich. It stands out from his other works because of the characters, which were quite unusual for their time. The twins are girls, rather than boys. They have a rather modern, single working mother and the father is blamed for the – provisional – failure of the parents' marriage.

5 places of
WORSHIP

476 SERVITINNEN

Herzogspitalstr. 9
Altstadt-Lehel ①
serviten.de/
servitinnen_muenchen/
anbetung.html

The Servite convent is tucked away in the heart of Munich's bustling old town. Since 1721, the Roman Catholic Sisters of the Blessed Sacrament honour the Lord, around the clock, with the support of various laymen. The church is open to the public. The nuns sell also candles, produced by themselves, in the tiny shop after Mass.

477 OST-WEST-FRIEDENSKIRCHE

Spiridon-Louis
Ring 100
Milbertshofen ④
ost-west-
friedenskirche.de

In the 1950s, a man came to Munich and built a church with his bare hands, using the piles of war rubble, inspired by an apparition of the Virgin Mary. The church is still here today. While it is not officially a church, it is a very spiritual place, a place to take a deep breath and reflect.

478 HERZ-JESU-KIRCHE

Lachnerstrasse 8
Neuhausen-
Nymphenburg ⑦
erzbistum-muenchen.
de/Pfarrei/Herz-Jesu-
Muenchen

Munich's most spectacular example of church architecture of the last twenty years. This Catholic church consists of a simple, open and light-filled room – a wooden box within a glass box – creating a flowing transition from the outside to the inside. The façade has floor-to-ceiling-high gates that can open out onto the church square.

479 OHEL-JAKOB-SYNAGOGE

Sankt-Jakobs-Platz 18
Altstadt-Lehel ⓘ
+49 (0)89 202 400 100
ikg-m.de/
juedisches-zentrum/
synagogenfuhrungen/

In 2006, Munich's new main synagogue was inaugurated. This spectacular building in the city centre can only be visited as part of a tour, for which you have to register at least 10 days in advance. Visitors can learn more about the history of the Jewish community in Munich, the synagogue's architecture and the services that are held there. Tours available in different languages.

480 FREIMANN-MOSCHEE

Wallnerstrasse 1
Fröttmaning
+49 (0)89 325 061

In Munich there are too few mosques. Bavaria's first mosque opened in 1973. It was built on the city's fringe, near the municipal sewage treatment plant. A good example of seventies-style architecture, that is firmly rooted in contemporary history and a dignified place of worship.

476 SERVITINNEN

5 helpful
WEBSITES & APPS

481 APP FOR NYMPHENBURG PALACE PARK

schloss-nymphenburg. de/englisch/park/ app.htm

This excellent app is your companion to the park, with plenty of historical information, audio documents, pictures and films. It also suggest routes you can follow so you don't get lost. It also features games children can play.

482 ARTS IN MUNICH

artsinmunich.com

An app about culture in Munich in its broadest sense. It tells you what is going on right now and next week, covering everything from gigs and exhibitions to restaurants, bars and hotels.

483 TOYTOWN GERMANY (MUNICH)

toytowngermany.com/ munich

An English-language community, where you can ask all sorts of questions about daily life in Munich, connect with others, and so on. They give you an expat's view on everyday life in Germany. Also a good read for Germans.

484 MUNIQUEANDO

muniqueando.com

Muniqueando started out in February 2012 as a small travel guide to Munich and the surrounding region, in Spanish. The blog gives travellers, as well as anyone who wants to make the most of his stay in the city, pointers on what to see and do.

485 PUBLIC PLAYGROUNDS

spielplatz-muenchen.de

If you are travelling with children, then you'll be relieved to find this website, which directs you to the nearest playground? You can filter +750 results by age and facilities. Plus, it's very helpful for grown-ups, too, as it also lists the fitness circuits for adults in the city.

5 hints for
PUBLIC TRANSPORT

486 INNENRAUM TICKET

Most of the stations you need on a tourist trip to Munich are located in the 'Innenraum' (inner district), the white zone on the coloured maps. You can buy a cheap day pass, called 'Single-Tageskarte Innenraum' or the 'Gruppen-Tageskarte Innenraum' for groups of up to five people. This is sufficient, unless you also want to go to the airport. You can buy tickets from the ticket vending machines in the stations or through the MVG Fahrinfo-app.

487 TICKET MACHINES

Why does Munich have so many different public transport tickets and ticket vending machines? There are blue and red machines, because the S-Bahn is operated by German railways (red), while the U-Bahn, bus and tram are operated by the city council (blue). But don't worry. If you buy your ticket on the U-Bahn, you can also use it on the S-Bahn (and vice versa), as long as you are in the matching tariff zone. Ask people if you're unsure, they'll be happy to help.

488 NACHTLINIEN

No matter where you go to a bar or disco, the theatre or the movies, the Nightlines, Munich's special bus and tram lines, which cover large parts of the city, will get you home safely. They all stop in Karlsplatz (Stachus) every hour on weekdays, every half-hour on the weekends, through the night. Public transport is usually very safe in Munich, by day or by night. Ask the drivers for assistance if you are uncertain which line to take.

489 BIKE TICKET

If you want to take a bike on the U-Bahn or S-Bahn (not on the tram or bus), then you have to buy a bicycle day pass (*Fahrrad-Tageskarte*) for three euro. Remember however that bikes are not allowed on the trains on weekdays between 6 to 8 am and 4 to 6 pm.

490 BUS X98

On weekends and public holidays, the express bus X98 departs directly from the main station to the 'flamingo entrance' of Tierpark Hellabrunn. It's very quick and convenient. This entrance is also more popular with the locals.

5 tips for
BMW LOVERS

---

491 BMW PLANT TOUR
Petuelring 130
Milbertshofen ④
+49 (0)89 125 016 001

Yes, you can tour the actual BMW plant. Book well in advance. You'll get to see all the production facilities of the BMW group plant – from the press shop to the assembly line. The tours are available in German and English and last approx. 2,5 hours.

492 BMW GROUP CLASSIC
Moosacher Strasse 6
Milbertshofen ④
+49 (0)89 125 016 001
bmwgroup-classic.com/
en/building.html

One of BMW's first production halls now houses the BMW brand's historic vehicle collection, the archive, the Classic Center and a historic workshop – all in one location. You can visit selected areas during guided tours. Book in advance by phone via the BMW Welt Info Service. There is also a cafe called Mo 66 on the premises.

493 NACHT DER WEISSEN HANDSCHUHE

**Am Olympiapark 2
Milbertshofen ④
*bmw-welt.com/de/
locations/museum.html***

During the so-called 'Night of the White Gloves' visitors of the BMW museum all wear white linen gloves and are finally allowed to do what is strongly discouraged on other days: stroke the cars they may usually caress with their eyes only. Get a feel for BMW's history.

494 DRIVENOW

drive-now.com/de/de

If you want to steer a BMW through town, the easiest way to do this is through their 'DriveNow' car sharing programme. Register in advance, ideally a few days before you want to hit the road. Check out their website for details.

495 BMW PAVILLON

**Lenbachplatz 7-A
Altstadt-Lehel ①
*bmw.de/de/topics/
faszination-bmw/
bmw-erleben/bmw-
lenbachplatz.html***

Built by Sep Ruf und Theo Pabst in the fifties, this BMW showroom was adapted to modern needs and is open every day. There are changing exhibitions and events. You can also register for DriveNow here.

5

UNIQUE THINGS

in Munich

496 **TAKING A RIDE IN A PATERNOSTER LIFT**
Blumenst rasse 28-B
Altstadt-Lehel ②

Munich's oldest skyscraper – a 1929 brick building with 12 floors – has a paternoster lift, which is still running to this day. Going up or down at a leisurely pace of 0,28 metres per second is an interesting experience. This is a public building the offices of the urban planning department – so you can take a ride in the lift during the opening hours.

497 **COWBOY CLUB**
Zentralländ-strasse 37
Thalkirchen ⑥
cowboyclub.de

In 1913, three craftsmen founded the Cowboy Club Munich because they would have liked to emigrate to the USA but did not have enough cash to do it. Here they cherished their American dream, met with like-minded people, and set up a ranch. In 1963, the club moved to new premises with a saloon, horses and tepees. You can visit the site during events like the annual open house.

498 ANATOMISCHE SCHAUSAMMLUNG

Pettenkoferstrasse 11
Ludwigsvorstadt ②
uni-muenchen.
de/einrichtungen/
sammlungen/
anatomische/
index.html

The Anatomical Collection is housed in an architectural gem. The building belongs to the university and the exhibits are open to non-students on Mondays. Here, you can see body parts, original preparations, historical models and models of organs.

499 ARCHIV GEIGER

Muttenthaler-
strasse 26
Solln
+49 (0)89 727 796 53
archiv-geiger.de

On the southern outskirts of the city you can visit the former studio of the artist Rupprecht Geiger, who created several major works for public spaces. He is best known for his colour field paintings, with lots of red tones. The studio is open to the public and is quite impressive.

500 REPTILIEN-AUFFANGSTATION

Kaulbachstrasse 37
Schwabing ③
+49 (0)89 218 050 30
reptilien
auffangstation.de

This volunteer association cares for reptiles that were given up by their owners or confiscated by the police or customs. The station takes in various animals including poisonous snakes or caimans. You can take a guided tour, to be booked in advance. This is not a visit to a clean terrarium, it's more of a peek into a habitat with a wild mix of species.

INDEX

COLOPHON

EDITING *and* COMPOSING — Judith Lohse

GRAPHIC DESIGN — Joke Gossé

PHOTOGRAPHY — Simone Schirmer

COVER IMAGE — Futuro House, Matti Suuronen, 1968
Part of Die Neue Sammlung — The Design Museum
Pinakotheken Area

The addresses in this book have been selected after thorough independent research
by the author, in collaboration with Luster Publishers. The selection is solely based
on personal evaluation of the business by the author. Nothing in this book was
published in exchange for payment or benefits of any kind.

D/2017/12.005/12

ISBN 978 94 6058 2301

NUR 512, 510

© 2018 Luster, Antwerp
www.lusterweb.com — www.the500hiddensecrets.com
info@lusterweb.com

Printed in Italy by Printer Trento.